How to Be a Happy,
HEALTHY
FAMILY

How to Be a Happy, HEALTHY FAMILY

Jim Burns, Ph.D.

WORD PUBLISHING

NASHVILLE

A Thomas Nelson Company

HOW TO BE A HAPPY, HEALTHY FAMILY

Unless otherwise indicated, Scripture quotations used in this book are from the Holy Bible, New International Version, copyright © 1973, 1978, 1984, International Bible Society. Used by permission of Zondervan Bible Publishers.

Other Scripture references are from the following sources:

The Message (MSG), copyright © 1993. Used by permission of NavPress Publishing Group.

The New King James Version (NKJV), copyright © 1979, 1980, 1982, Thomas Nelson, Inc., Publishers.

The New Revised Standard Version of the Bible (NRSV), copyright © 1989 by the Division of Christian Education of the National Council of the Churches of Christ in the USA.

Published in association with Yates & Yates, LLP, Literary Agents, Orange, California.

Library of Congress Cataloging-in-Publication Data

Burns, Jim, 1953–
    How to be a happy, healthy family / by Jim Burns.
        p. cm.
    Includes bibliographical references.
    ISBN 0-8499-4269-1
    1. Family—Religious life. 2. Parenting—Religious aspects—Christianity. I. Title.
    BV4526.3 .B87 2001
    248.8'45—dc21   2001026270
                                                       CIP

Printed in the United States of America

01 02 03 04 05 06 PHX 6 5 4 3 2 1

For Cathy

You continue to amaze me and inspire me.
Thank you for your sacrificial example of making our family
your priority.

CONTENTS

ACKNOWLEDGMENTS

SPECIAL THANKS TO

Carrie Hicks Steele—you constantly work far above and beyond the call of duty. You are a blessing and a gift sent straight from God.

The incredible YouthBuilders staff—you are constantly making a positive impact in the world of family-based youth ministry. I am honored to work side by side with you.

Christy, Rebecca, and Heidi Burns—you bring me the greatest joy in my life. What a delight and privilege to be your dad.

Dr. Jon Wallace—you are an inspirational friend and hero.

Sealy Yates, Tom Thompson, and Joey Paul—thank you for believing in this message and the messenger. I am grateful.

And a very special thank-you to the board of directors of Youth-Builders as well as the thousands of supporters and friends who have helped create this worldwide grass-roots movement of family-based youth ministry. You are making a difference.

INTRODUCTION

THE DAY OUR OLDEST DAUGHTER, Christy, arrived home from the hospital, I panicked. How do I hold her? How do I change her? What do we do with her for the next fifty years? Today she is a teenager, and I'm still panicked.

Parenting isn't easy. In fact, it is humbling. Parenting has brought out the very best and the very worst in me. If you are having an easy time as a parent, then something is probably wrong. Yes, our children have brought Cathy and me closer together than we ever imagined and, yes, our strongest disagreements have come to us compliments of having children.

Christy Meredith Burns arrived at six pounds and ten ounces. No one had sent us to "parenting school," so we started making up what to do and how to react. The problem was that we came from typical dysfunctional families and found ourselves copying behavior we had actually resented growing up. We decided we needed help. Cathy and I had degrees in child development or youth and family ministry, but we were still lost.

So we came up with a great idea. We would look for lessons from mentors. We examined the finest books on family written during the past twenty-five years. We interviewed hundreds of couples and young people. We dialogued with colleagues. What came out of our search is this simple parenting book. As we explored high and low for the right way to parent, we learned two very important things: (1) there is no perfect method to parenting, and (2) most parents are doing a very adequate job of parenting but don't know it. We have concluded that there are basically ten essential ingredients for a happy, healthy family.

In my own writing and speaking work, I have focused most often on families and kids in crisis. Sometimes the news media can be extremely negative when it comes to families and children. However, there is some very good news that often gets missed by the newsmakers. Thousands upon thousands of families around the world are thriving and working positively through their issues. Many parents are becoming the transitional generation for their children. These parents came from dysfunctional homes; they experienced and inherited some of their problems from the previous generation. But they are breaking the chain of dysfunction and working hard at parenting their children in a more positive environment. The result will be children who will be more secure and have a legacy of love and health passed on to the next generation.

Join us on our continued journey as we look at *How to Be a Happy, Healthy Family*. Cathy and I will be the first to tell you that no family is perfect. Our three children will be the next to agree that our family has a long way to go, but we're on this journey together. Let's look at the ten basic steps to creating a more healthy and positive family environment.

THE YOUTHBUILDERS
HEALTHY FAMILY COVENANT

- *The Power of Being There*
  Your children regard your very presence as a sign of caring and connectedness.
- *Express Affection, Warmth, and Encouragement*
  A family with a sense of A.W.E. as opposed to shame-based parenting is a home where children and spouses will feel more secure.
- *Build Healthy Morals and Values*
  The decisions kids make today will often affect them for the rest of their lives.
- *Discipline with Consistency*
  Clearly expressed expectations and consistent follow-through produce responsible kids.
- *Ruthlessly Eliminate Stress*
  The unbalanced life will not be kind to the areas we neglect.
- *Communication Is the Key*
  Positive communication is the language of love for our children.
- *Play Is Necessary for a Close-Knit Family*
  There is nothing like play to bring about family togetherness and communication.
- *Love Your Spouse*
  A loving marriage brings hope and security to the children.
- *The Best Things in Life Are Not Things*
  Healthy stewardship and financial decisions produce positive family priorities.
- *Energize Your Family's Spiritual Growth*
  Your greatest calling in life is to leave a spiritual legacy for your children.

1

THE POWER OF
BEING THERE

My mom died a few years ago. It wasn't easy. Cancer racked her body, and we spent most of a year watching her die.

We had moved Mom home from the hospital and were trying to make her as comfortable as possible with hospice care. We moved a hospital bed into Mom and Dad's bedroom. I would often find myself sitting on their bed while she lay in her hospital bed.

One day she was dozing and very weak, when all of a sudden she perked up and asked me, "Jimmy, where is your dad?"

"He's watching a baseball game on TV. Do you need him, Mom?"

"No, not really," she replied. Then she looked up at me and said, "You know, Jimmy, I never really liked baseball."

"You never liked baseball, Mom?" I was puzzled. "Did you ever miss a Little League game of mine?"

"No."

"Did you miss any of my Pony League, junior high, or high school games, Mom?"

Again she replied, "I don't think so."

"Mom," I continued, "you never missed a game, and on top of that you never missed any of my three brothers' games either. Dad and you watch ball games all day long on TV. What do you mean you never liked baseball?"

"Jimmy, I didn't go to the games to watch baseball. I went to the games to be with you!"

I realized at that moment the reason this incredible woman had such a powerful impact on my life was because of the power of being there even when she didn't care for the activity. Her very presence in my life was cause for great inspiration and influence. She taught me the power of being there.

YOUR CHILDREN REGARD YOUR VERY PRESENCE as a sign of caring and connectedness. The power of being there makes a difference in a child's life. This sounds so simple, but don't underestimate the positive message you are giving your kids by watching those games, driving them all around the county, or the hundreds of other ways you are present in their lives. You don't have to be physically present with your kids 24/7, but your presence in their lives gives them a greater sense of security than almost any other quality you can offer them. All studies on positive family living tell us that the results are well worth it when families engage in meaningful times together. Soccer moms, it's worth it. Dads who leave work early to watch the game, it's worth it. Single parents, as tired as you may be, if you continue to find the time to go on special outings with your kids, you will reap the benefits now *and* later in your family life.

Here are a few things I have learned about parenting during the past sixteen years:

Parenting isn't easy. If you are having an easy go at it, then something is probably wrong. Parenting is exhausting. Just ask the mother of a newborn—or a two-year-old, a ten-year-old, or even a sixteen-year-old, for that matter!

Parenting is frustrating. We still live in a make-believe world in which some of us actually expect that there is a place this side of heaven where no conflict resides. If there is such a place, it isn't in the family.

Parenting is delayed gratification. Parents plant seeds in their children that will not sprout until adulthood. Parenting is partnering with God to bring his children into the world and then helping him make them all they were meant to be.

Parenting is the highest calling on earth. There is no doubt that one of the primary reasons God placed you on this planet was to pass on a positive, healthy legacy to your family.

The crazy thing about parenting is that there is no single method or plan that works perfectly and no guarantee that if what you are doing is working with kid number one that it will work with kids number two, three, four, or however many kids you are brave enough to have. You can debate the various philosophies of parenting and family life. Believe me, there are hundreds—no, thousands—of parenting plans out there. Many of them actually contradict each other! However, all healthy parenting plans will tell you, in one way or the other, that when parenting is placed in its simplest form, happy, healthy families experience the power of being there for each other. Most parents reading this book are doing a much better job than they would actually believe and, although the results are long-term, their investment of time, attention, and very presence in the lives of their children will make a positive difference.

Your job as a parent is a calling from God. It is more important than your vocation, bank account, education, or even your own happiness. Besides your relationship with God himself, your influence and impact with your children is primary and will no doubt be your greatest legacy.

Throughout the Bible, family and children are the priority. Jesus was in a slight disagreement with his disciples when he showed them his high priority for children. Let's look into the heart of God when it comes to children:

> People were bringing little children to Jesus to have him touch them, but the disciples rebuked them. When Jesus saw this, he was indignant. He said to them, "Let the little children come to me, and do not hinder them, for the kingdom of God belongs to such as these. I tell you the truth, anyone who will not receive the kingdom of God like a little child will never enter it." And he took the children in his arms, put his hands on them and blessed them. (Mark 10:13–16)

On another occasion, Jesus was discussing the priority of children with his disciples, but the disciples kept interrupting him and wanting to talk about "more important" issues. However, Jesus gently kept bringing them back to lessons on children. Look at Mark 9:36–37:

> He [Jesus] took a little child and had him stand among them. Taking him in his arms, he said to them [the disciples], "Whoever welcomes one of these little children in my name welcomes me; and whoever welcomes me does not welcome me but the one who sent me."

When you welcome a child, you welcome Jesus. How's that for priority? The first time I spoke to people in Guatemala, I met one of the most radiant women I will ever meet. Halfway through the first general session, she appeared in the back of the hall. She wore a colorful Indian skirt, hand-embroidered blouse, beads, and a brilliant smile from ear to ear. She was probably about four feet eleven inches by four feet eleven inches!

I asked my interpreter Jeffrey DeLeon, "Who is the incredible woman who came in halfway through the first presentation?" I had noticed that he had nodded to her.

He answered, "Oh, she is a saint. She lives in a mountainous section of our country and may be the only person in her area within hundreds of miles who works with children and youth. She probably rode on a bus at least twelve hours all night to get here. She is an exceptional woman."

"I want to meet her," I replied. He then told me that her twelve-year-old son had died about three months earlier. I asked him, "How does she do it? How does she still manage to work with kids? I think I would be curled up in the fetal position if something like that ever happened to me." He encouraged me to go ask her.

I walked up to her, and we connected even though we didn't know each other's language very well. I said, "Lo siento." *I'm sorry.* She nodded as if she understood. I then asked in the most broken Spanish known to humankind, "How do you manage to still work with kids when your own son died just three months ago?" She smiled although there was grief in her eyes and said, "Porque los niños están más cerca del corazón de Dios," *Because children are closest to the heart of God.*

She was right. When Jesus said, "When you welcome a child you welcome me," he was clearly communicating that your role as a parent is a most important calling. We can see how close children are to the heart of God when we see Jesus get angry. One of the few times in the Bible we see Jesus' anger is his response to the wrongful treatment of children. Look at these strong words of Jesus: "And if anyone causes one of these little ones who believe in me to sin, it would be better for him to be thrown into the sea with a large millstone tied around his neck" (Mark 9:42).

We have a friend who chose to be a stay-at-home mom. She is lovely and brilliant, and she sacrificed a great deal of money to make the choice of staying at home. Her husband was a professor at a prestigious university on the East Coast. Recently, she told my wife, Cathy, and me that she was always intimidated by faculty social gatherings. People would turn to her and ask, "And what is it that you do, my dear?" At first she would sheepishly say something like, "Oh, I'm just a mom." The response was usually, "Oh, that's nice." That is, until our friend Peggy came up with a new line: "I am socializing two Homo sapiens into the dominant values of the Judeo-Christian tradition in order that they might be the instruments for the transformation of the social order into the kind of eschatological utopia that God willed from the beginning of creation!" Peggy's description of parenting reminds us that, whether we choose to stay at home with our children or work outside the home, our true vocation is to develop a happy, healthy family; whatever else we do is secondary.

I have the privilege to speak and listen to thousands of young people each year. The number one request from kids for their parents is for a relationship with them. They seek their parents' time and attention. Please never underestimate the power of being there in your child's life. Two key points to remember are (1) bless your kids with your presence, and (2) bless your kids with affection.

BLESS YOUR KIDS WITH YOUR PRESENCE

You are probably doing this already and doing it well. In reality, moms often do better than dads. Dads sometimes get sidetracked. My daughter Rebecca reminded me of the power of being there when she was in third grade. One night at dinner she announced to the family that I was coming to Mrs. Saxe's third-grade class for her "show and tell" time. Rebecca didn't ask; she told us. I asked her if the other daddies were being invited to come to class.

She said, "No, Dad, just you."

I replied, "Don't you usually share a book or a doll or pictures?"

She answered, "Usually, Dad, but not on Tuesday. I promised my teacher you would come."

"What if I can't come that day?"

"Then you'll need to change your schedule. I promised my teacher!"

"Rebecca, do you want me to bring my résumé?"

"What's a résumé?"

"It lists all the important things mommies and daddies do."

"No, don't bring that. I'd be embarrassed."

"Do you want me to bring the book I wrote and dedicated to you?"

"No, Dad. Don't bring the book. Just relax and bring yourself!"

So I agreed to go to her class, without anything to impress her fellow third graders.

On that Tuesday I spoke to thirty-five hundred high school students at an assembly on drug and alcohol abuse. No problem. That's what I'm comfortable doing. But as I drove to Rebecca's class I grew more and more nervous. Would the kids like me? I didn't want to embarrass Rebecca. What could I say to a bunch of third graders? I arrived at her school a bit early and walked to Rebecca's class. I figured I would sit in the back and get comfortable with the kids while Mrs. Saxe was teaching the class.

As I opened the door, every eye turned toward me and away from Mrs. Saxe as she was teaching math. She pointed for me to go the back of the room and wait. (I had been sent to the back of the room other times when I was in school, but for a different reason!) While Mrs. Saxe continued her teaching, Rebecca stood up and interrupted the class, walked over to me, and took my hand, saying, "Come on, Dad. It's your turn." I tried to whisper that Mrs. Saxe was not ready for me, but it didn't matter to Rebecca. She pulled me to the front of the class, pushing Mrs. Saxe out of the way. The teacher smiled and reluctantly canceled the remainder of the math lesson for the day.

Rebecca introduced me to the class. "This is my dad. His name is Jim. He is a great guy and he's bald." As if they hadn't noticed!

I spoke for five minutes and made a beeline to the door. Mrs. Saxe stopped me and said, "Dr. Burns, perhaps some of the children have questions for you." I'm thinking, *Right, third graders have questions for me.* Dozens of hands shot up. I pointed to Matthew. "Do you have a question, Matt?"

"Yeah, how old are you anyway? You look kind of old to be Rebecca's dad."

With my self-image slipping, I told him my age. He just shook his head. I had never thought of myself as old until that moment! I needed encouragement, so I turned to Rebecca's good friend Mallory. "Yes, Mallory?"

"Jim," she began, letting the rest of the kids know that we were on a first-name basis, "do you own a dog?"

"Well, uh, Mallory, of course, you know that we, uh, do not own a dog." I was caught in a setup, and it didn't matter that I told the class we had other animals.

Mallory looked around the room for support and shouted back, "Rebecca wants a dog!" I sank deeper. (Incidentally, today Rebecca has a beautiful golden retriever that I feed, walk, and clean up after.) The questions continued one after another. None of the kids asked about my educational background or salary or any of the things that we adults often place on the pedestal of importance. The kids mainly asked relational questions.

When I was finally finished with the last question, again I headed for the door. This time Rebecca stood up and came toward me. I thought, *Oh, no. What now?* She reached her arms around me with a big hug and simply said, "Daddy, thank you for coming to class today. I am so proud of you."

Rebecca and her third-grade class didn't see my tears, but I cried all the way to my car. It had dawned on me that Rebecca doesn't care about academic degrees, awards, credentials, or even money (although she wants hundred-dollar Nike Airs right now); she cares about relationships. She wants my time and attention and my presence. Her security does not come from my work; it comes from my presence. Our children crave the power of being there, and nothing can make up for our presence. Additionally, children tell me they not only want our attention, but they also desire our affection.

BLESS YOUR KIDS WITH AFFECTION

Researchers tell us that we need eight to ten meaningful touches a day to thrive. Many children—and adults, for that matter—are starved for healthy, positive, appropriate, physical attention. Dr. Ross Campbell, M.D., claims, "In all my research and experience I have never known of one sexually disoriented person who had a warm, loving and affectionate father."

The power of being there is more than just our presence; it is also our touch and affection. Do your kids know you love them? Of course they do. But they still need a hug and a verbal "I love you" on a daily basis. If you didn't come from a family that displayed affection, then you might have more difficulty with being affectionate, but your children still need the reassurance and blessing of your affection.

I once wrote a book to students on the topic of sex and dating. Immediately the calls started coming in, usually from mothers who were nervous about their children. They wanted me to meet with their teenagers and fix any problem they were having with their sexuality and relationships. This, of course, was ludicrous; but during that season of my life I met some of the most persistent parents in the world. One mother of a seventeen-year-old, sexually promiscuous daughter called at least twenty times, and my assistant finally pleaded with me to take the appointment so she could quit spending so much time on the phone with this mother.

On the day of their arrival we were all a bit curious to see what was going to happen. I must admit how surprised I was to meet two of the nicest parents I had ever met and a beautiful girl with a very pleasing personality. Through our conversation, I confirmed that the girl had become quite sexually active. She was a Christian and felt some remorse, but I really couldn't get to the core of the issue. I asked the mom and dad to step out of my office because I wanted to talk with the daughter by herself. She was pleasant and willing to talk, but she didn't want to talk about her sexuality. She wanted to talk about her father.

She said, "I used to be so close to my dad. When I was younger, he would play with me and toss me in the air. I would snuggle on his lap, and he would read to me and do magic tricks. When he would come home from work, he would always give me a hug and say 'How's my little princess?'" Then her lip began to quiver, and she looked away from me, saying, "I guess I'm not his little princess anymore."

I had heard enough. I brought the mom and the dad back into the room. I asked the dad, "How's your relationship with your daughter?" He looked over at her with obvious love and the first hint of tenderness I had seen from him and said, "We used to be close. I would play with her and read to her and pick her up in the air and call her my little princess." Now it was his turn for his lip to quiver. Maybe it was hereditary! He looked at me and added, "Then when she got to be about thirteen, her body started changing as well as her attitude, and it was just more difficult."

I looked him right in the eyes and said, "My friend, if you don't take the time to hug your daughter with appropriate hugs often, there are hundreds of boys who would love to hug her with inappropriate hugs and more." She needed to be his little princess now more than ever.

Children need to experience touch and affection from their parents or they will look for a counterfeit as they get older. Jesus took the little children in his arms and blessed them. Touch is a major form of blessing. In the Bible when parents blessed a child, they very often placed loving hands on the child and embraced them. There is power in touch. If you come from a home where you did not receive much affection or touch, then it may be difficult for you to pour on the affection. You don't need to move from stoic to mushy, but there is a happy medium where you may have to stretch your comfort level for the sake of your children.

After a seminar one man told me, "You just don't understand how difficult it is for me to hold my three children. I grew up in a home where my very formal parents never hugged us kids. My dad showed his love by working hard and bringing home an excellent paycheck, and my mom showered her love on us with wonderful home-cooked meals." I think he was looking for me to excuse him.

I replied, "I'm very sorry that you did not receive the power of physical touch in your home growing up, and yet it sounds like you came from a home where your parents did the best they could do." He nodded in agreement.

I continued, "Now you can be the transitional generation and pass on to your children the love you received from your parents *and* the power of touch. No one said parenting would be easy, but you now know better. It will get easier."

His wife smiled and said, "He's going to need quite a bit of practice."

"Great," I agreed. Turning back toward the man, I said, "It sounds like you have three little ones you can 'practice' with and probably your wife could use a hug more often also." His wife nodded in agreement. I'd bet everyone in his family received a hug that day.

The power of being there for our children is so profoundly meaningful that we often miss it. When kids understand that their parents are there for them, they can overcome amazing obstacles and circumstances to make a positive impact in their world. The power of being there is a deposit into a child's emotional, physical, and spiritual bank account that will bring intimacy and understanding to a family. Many times parents look for the latest parenting fad to become a close-knit family. Yet the answer is simple and right in front of them. It's investing our time and energy and commitment to be there for our children. The result is hope and security for all.

In 1989, an earthquake in what was then Soviet Armenia took only four minutes to flatten the nation and kill more than thirty thousand people. Here's how Max Lucado described this most moving story:

> Moments after the deadly tremor ceased, a father raced to an elementary school to save his son. When he arrived, he saw that the building had been leveled. Looking at the mass of stones and rubble, he remembered a promise he had made to his child: *"No matter what happens, I'll always be there for you."* Driven by his own promise, he found the area

closest to his son's room and began to pull back the rocks. Other parents arrived and began sobbing for their children. "It's too late," they told the man. "You know they are dead. You can't help." Even a police officer encouraged him to give up.

But the father refused. For eight hours, then sixteen hours, then thirty-two, thirty-six hours he dug. His hands were raw and his energy gone, but he refused to quit. Finally after thirty-eight wrenching hours, he pulled back a boulder and heard his son's voice. He called his boy's name. "Arman! Arman!" And a voice answered, "Dad, it's me." The boy added these priceless words, "I told the other kids not to worry. I told them if you were alive, you'd save me and when you saved me, they'd be saved too. Because you promised, *No matter what I'll always be there for you.*"[1]

FURTHER READING

• Trent, John. *Be There!* Colorado Springs: WaterBrook, 2000.

John Trent is one of my favorite authors and communicators. For more information about his writing and seminars, contact Encouraging Words, 1629 N. Tatum Blvd., Suite 208, Phoenix, AZ 85032. www.EncouragingWords.com

DISCUSSION STARTERS

1. When you were a child, did you experience the power of being there and/or the power of affection from your parents?

2. Use the following scale to rate your own parenting with your child/children:

THE POWER OF BEING THERE

1	2	3	4	5
needs immediate attention		so-so		great

THE POWER OF AFFECTION

1	2	3	4	5
needs immediate attention		so-so		great

3. "Your children regard your very presence as a sign of caring and connectedness." How do you interpret this statement?

4. What do you see as the significant message of Jesus' words and actions in the following verses?

People were bringing little children to Jesus to have him touch them, but the disciples rebuked them. When Jesus saw this, he was indignant. He said to them, "Let the little children come to me, and do not hinder them, for the kingdom of God belongs to such as these. I tell you the truth, anyone who will not receive the kingdom of God like a little child will never enter it." And he took the children in his arms, put his hands on them and blessed them. (Mark 10:13–16)

He took a little child and had him stand among them. Taking him in his arms, he said to them, "Whoever welcomes one of these little children in my name welcomes me; and whoever welcomes me does not welcome me but the one who sent me." (Mark 9:36–37)

And if anyone causes one of these little ones who believe in me to sin, it would be better for him to be thrown into the sea with a large millstone tied around his neck. (Mark 9:42)

Need some practical ideas on spending time with your children? Here's a list created by children ages six to eighteen on ideas they would like to do with their parent or parents:

1. Daily phone calls
2. Weekly dates
3. Special traditions
4. Attend the games and plays
5. Drive to school
6. Puzzles
7. Special TV program with popcorn
8. Notes
9. Take them on a business trip
10. Photography lessons
11. Play tennis
12. Skip rocks and have a contest
13. Write a letter to God
14. Walk the dog
15. Read a good book together
16. Go out for breakfast or doughnuts
17. Take pictures
18. Go to the park
19. Visit the library and ask the librarian a bizarre question
20. Develop a new laugh together
21. Visit the zoo
22. Visit a museum
23. Ride bikes
24. Learn a hobby
25. Wash a car
26. Rollerblade
27. Climb a tree
28. Climb a mountain
29. Eat creatively one whole day for $1.29
30. Picnic
31. Shop for cars
32. Go to the airport and watch people
33. Visit the beach or lake
34. Ice-skate
35. Shop
36. Play backgammon
37. Go horseback riding
38. Play pinball
39. Hit golf balls or play miniature golf
40. Bowl
41. Water sports
42. Fly a kite
43. Go on a hike
44. Plant a garden together
45. Play board games or card games
46. Fish
47. Sail
48. Play tennis
49. Play croquet
50. Go river rafting or tubing
51. Play badminton
52. Build a tree house
53. Go to a casual dinner but dress up
54. Make homemade ice cream
55. Bake cookies
56. Attend a play
57. Go to the movies
58. Go to a sports event
59. Visit a swap meet or a garage sale
60. Feed ducks
61. Go to the circus
62. Go to the county fair
63. Volunteer at a soup kitchen

2

EXPRESS AFFECTION, WARMTH, AND ENCOURAGEMENT

I didn't meet Rob Thibaut until he was forty-three, and he died when he was fifty. Many men don't have what you would call a best friend. But from the first time I met Rob, he took over a major place in my heart. We met at a church where I was speaking in Maui. He handed me his business card and asked if we could meet to talk about his relationship with his daughter. Our family was in Hawaii on a three-month sabbatical and I almost turned him down, but something told me that it would be a special meeting. It was.

I counseled him, but somehow this man gave me an amazing amount of strength and energy. We continued to meet while I was in Maui, sometimes socially and sometimes to talk over family issues. What makes this guy tick? *I wondered.*

After my first meeting with Rob, I pulled out his business card. He was the president of a successful restaurant chain in Hawaii and California that soon became my favorite. He told me later that he was on President Gerald Ford's foundation board. I was amazed how many movie stars he knew and could only imagine that his bank account was quite comfortable. Usually people like that intimidated me, but Rob didn't. He put the same amount of love and energy into the dishwashers at his restaurant as he did with ex–presidents of the United States.

He rapidly moved from counselee to friend, mentor, teacher. What is it about this man? I asked myself.

It wasn't until the night Rob told me he was going to die that I figured it out. I "happened" to be in Maui one night after my family had returned home before flying to Honolulu to speak at a conference. I had a message on my voice mail at the hotel from Rob, whom I planned to see the next day. He said, "Jimmy, I can't meet with you tomorrow. I'm in the hospital, and the doctor just told me I don't have long to live. I'm worried about Patty and the kids. Will you check in with them for me? I love you, and aloha, Jim." I sat stunned on the edge of my bed in the hotel room and then literally ran to my car to drive to the other side of the island to sit with Rob at the hospital. Patty had just left for the night, and Rob was all alone.

We talked for two hours about his love for his beautiful wife, Patty, and his three incredible kids. He shared about each child one at a time and told me his favorite family stories. Almost like the prophets of the Old Testament, he blessed his children one by one. We talked about his dad, his work, his friends, and his faith. I read scriptures to him. That night, Rob and I prayed together, held each other, and cried.

A week later Cathy and I sat at Rob's funeral or, more appropriate, celebration. It was a mix of Hawaiian hula and song, strong Christian testimony, and a lovely tribute to a wonderful husband, father, and friend. As we all boarded boats to pay our respects for the last time on the water near his beloved Napili Bay, Maui, it finally hit me. Rob treated all people in his presence as if they were special guests at a party in their honor. He didn't complain or nag or whine. Sure, he was a realist, but he empowered and validated our worth through a positive spirit even when he knew he was dying. He was a great man who empowered people through affirmation, warmth, and encouragement.

If the love and respect we gather in a lifetime is the measure of a man, Rob will be remembered for a long, long while. He was a positive encouragement to so many people. He always had time for each individual and made everyone feel special. At his fiftieth birthday bash a few months before he died, he was best friend, best man, mentor, parent, or partner to half the people attending. He was the most generous and loving of men I have ever known. I miss you, Rob.

MARY STRUGGLED IN HER ROLE AS A PARENT. It wasn't because she didn't love her kids or put in the effort. If anything, Mary tried too hard and took the role of parenting more seriously than humanly possible. Her relationship with her husband, Jerry, was suffering, partly due to the fact that she was just too overwhelmed with all the energy she expended on the all-consuming role of mother. She told me once that one of her boys said, "You think you are a good mommy, but you really aren't." Ouch! Yet there might have been a hint of truth in that statement. It wasn't because she neglected her boys, far from it. Rather, she had no life besides her children. She was using the same dysfunctional parenting philosophy her dysfunctional parents used with her.

Mary didn't come from an Ozzie and Harriet family. Her mom was pregnant with her at age seventeen, and her dad was forced into a "shotgun wedding." Her grandma struggled emotionally, her mom struggled with depression, and now she struggled, period. Coming from a dysfunctional home, Mary battled a low self-image and an extremely negative spirit, which she unleashed regularly on her boys and her husband. We talked because she sensed that things were spiraling more and more out of control with her teenage son and mentioned that she and her husband were really at odds with each other. She told me that she and her husband didn't have the emotional strength to work on the marriage, but she was looking for insight with her son.

I asked the whole family to come in and get acquainted. Quickly, the session went sour with everyone ganging up on Mary. She was "too controlling," "too negative," "inconsistent with discipline," nag, nag, nag. Mary had tears in her eyes. She had learned to be a pretty tough character and, because of her unhealthy family background, her response was to get defensive. She fought back. In a very controlled manner she told me each of the children's bad sides and took her husband to task for lots of little issues. I'm sure what she said was mostly true. The family went silent. Mary had won the battle. The children and husband were embarrassed and shamed by Mary's criticism.

Mary had won the battle, but she was losing the war. Why? Shame-based parenting and negativity simply does not work in the long run. Mary's grandma had tried it on her mother, her mom used shame-based parenting as the primary way to communicate with her, and now she used it on her family. Just as it hadn't worked for the previous generations, it wasn't going to work in Mary's family. It was Abraham Maslow, the great Jewish thinker, who said that for every one critical statement we give to another person, it takes nine affirming statements to make up for it. Tragically, shame-based parenting has been perhaps the most dominant style of parenting for the past several centuries. It didn't work for Mary's mother and it didn't work for Mary, but for some reason, we still use and abuse it.

You may have grown up in a home like Mary's. And you may be asking, "Fine, but what parenting strategy does work?" In a later conversation with Mary, very much aware of her fragile self-image, I said, "At the risk of doing a bit of damage to our friendship, let me say that nagging, overcontrol, negativity, and shame-based parenting will get you the initial victory, but unless you make some serious changes and decisions, your relationship with your children is headed down the same path as your relationship with your mother and grandmother. Mary, are you willing to work as hard as you have ever worked to reestablish and restructure your style of parenting with your kids and the way you relate to your husband?"

She didn't answer my question; instead, she was hurting so badly she decided to tell me a few more zingers about her children and husband. I said, "Did you hear what you just did? You didn't answer my question; you gave out more ammunition to let me know how hard it is being married to Jerry and how difficult your kids are. You've convinced me *they* are challenging. But what about you?" Mary began to cry.

PARENTING WITH A.W.E. (AFFIRMATION, WARMTH, ENCOURAGEMENT)

Cathy and I were able to introduce Mary to a different style of parenting and, frankly, relating to people in general. We call it parenting with A.W.E. The A.W.E stands for affirmation, warmth, and encouragement. Of course, this is easier said than done when we are in the midst of the battle and feel that we are losing ground. It is amazing how easy it is to revert back to the old ways of shame-based parenting, especially since the short-term results of shame-based parenting are evident immediately and the long-term results of A.W.E. often come after a harvest of progress.

Many parenting experts talk about a child's emotional bank account.

Using this analogy, shame-based parenting usually takes out many more withdrawals than deposits. Although this may sound like an over-simplification, shame-based parenting focuses on withdrawals, while A.W.E.–based parenting concentrates on placing deposits in the emotional bank account. Joe White, president of Kanakuk-Kanakomo Kamps and all-around great guy, did an incredible thing at a Promise Keepers' event where we both spoke recently. He threw out in the arena one bag of red beans and one bag of white beans. He challenged the men to try an experiment for a month: Every time they took a withdrawal from their wife's emotional bank account, they should put a red bean in the jar; and every time they made a deposit, they should place a white bean in another jar. After a month, they were to look at the jars and measure how they did.

Shame-based parenting uses words and actions that cause kids to think they aren't loved or valuable. Shame-based is performance-oriented and approval-focused. Kids from shame-based homes say it was *never* good enough for Dad, or Mom used to say things like "Can't you do anything right?" and "Just let me do it so it gets done on time." Those are words that win the battle but lose the war.

A.W.E.–based parenting makes our children feel loved and accepted even in the midst of discipline. I love the plaque I have hanging on the wall in my office, which says: "Every child needs someone who is irrationally positive about them." Kids who live in an environment of affirmation, warmth, and encouragement feel listened to and appreciated. These kids have the confidence to go out and take on life because they know their parents believe in them, value them, and enjoy them. Cathy and I need lots of reminders to drop the old style and pick up the right way to parent. Here's our A.W.E. reminder list:

DEPOSITS

- Say "I'm sorry" to your children when you blow it
- Praise often
- Believe the best of them
- Forgive them
- Hug often
- Say "I love you" every day
- Write thank-you and love notes
- Pray for them
- Speak with a tender tone and voice
- Brag about them
- Spend time playing together
- Listen to them because listening is the language of love
- Take special dates and time together

WITHDRAWALS

- Nagging
- Belittling them
- Sarcasm
- Negative put-downs
- Critical spirit

- Hypercritical living

- Screaming

- Never saying "I'm sorry"

- Fighting constantly with your spouse

- Talking about them negatively to others

- Favoritism

- Silence

- Heaping guilt on them

- Being rude and irritable

Parenting with A.W.E. means parenting with affirmation, warmth, and encouragement. It doesn't mean that we remove discipline, but it does mean we try our best to remove shaming our children into making the right decisions. If we would only work as hard at creating a warm, loving environment of affection and affirmation with our family as many of us do in our vocation, we would have a better family atmosphere. Here's what it will take to parent your children with A.W.E.

AFFIRMATION

Believe in your children. Most young people struggle with a poor or improper self-image. They play the comparison game and see that someone is always smarter, prettier, more coordinated, and richer than they are. They need someone in their lives who believes in them even when they can't believe in themselves on their own. Don't forget this:

The difference between kids who make it and kids who don't most often is one caring adult.

Jesus met a fisherman named Simon, and early in their relationship he nicknamed him Petras (Peter). Petras means "rock." Yes, Jesus nicknamed him Rocky. Jesus even gave a wordplay on Peter's name when he pointed to Simon Peter and said, "On this rock I will build my church" (Matt. 16:18). Who became the leader of the early church? It was Simon, the stumbling, bumbling fisherman who became Peter, the rock-solid leader of the early church. Parents must pray for the same power Jesus had to believe in their children and help build up their shaky self-images to become all God has in store for them to be.

Shower your children with praise. Mark Twain once said, "I can live two months on one good compliment." Praise and affirmation are positive, motivating factors. Negative put-downs are deflating. Praise your kids, but don't lie to them; there is a difference. If my parents had told me that I was the best-looking boy at Fremont Junior High, I would have known they were lying! The next time they praised me I would have questioned their sincerity. Vain flattery is an emotional withdrawal, but true, meaningful praise will be a major deposit in your children's emotional bank accounts. Praise your children often, and praise their inner qualities as well as outer ones.

Be available. It's back to the power of being there for your kids. A recent study on kids who are prone to drug and alcohol abuse showed that if a family has dinner together several nights a week, their children will be less likely to be involved in drug or alcohol abuse. Your very presence in their life makes a difference.

Nene, my grandma, was one of the major heroes of my life. At eighty-seven, she was deteriorating physically and mentally due to Alzheimer's disease. Sometimes she recognized me and sometimes she didn't. I never dreamed she would live to see the birth of our last child, but she did. She was even able to come to the baby shower. I have a picture of Nene holding our youngest daughter, Heidi—both have dazed looks on their faces. I treasure that picture to this day.

When it was time to open the presents at our baby shower, my brother Bill went over to help Nene out of her chair. I happened to be walking by when he said, "Come on, Nene, let's go watch Jim and Cathy open those gifts for their new baby, Heidi."

Dazed and confused, she said, "Who?"

He shouted in her ear (she was also hearing impaired), "Jim and Cathy have a new baby, and we are going to open some gifts. Come on, I'll help you up."

Frustrated and in pain, she told Bill, "I can't get up. I didn't buy them a present. I'm tired, I'm old, and I just want to die."

Bill gently replied, "Nene, I don't think anyone is concerned that you didn't purchase a gift."

At that point I walked up to my dear, loving grandma and said, "Nene, your very presence in the room makes a difference to me. For all my life just your presence has given me strength."

Nene died shortly after the baby shower. She never really had much money, but it was never her gifts that made a difference; it was her very presence and availability that still give me strength today.

WARMTH

Create a home environment of warmth and affection. You may be saying, "But you don't understand who I am married to" or "My adolescent isn't exactly the perfect example of love, affection, and devotion." I'm sure you're right. So start with yourself and, in the words of Bill Murray in the hilarious movie *What about Bob?* take "baby steps." Taking baby steps means that if you have twenty things to go over with your teenager when he or she gets home from school, and most of the agenda deals with things your teenager should have done but didn't—wait. Don't go over anything in your agenda. Take your child out for his or her favorite junk food. Don't bring up any problems; instead, spend your time listening to whatever your child wants to talk about. Ask no probing questions; make no accusations. Talk with your child the way his or her friends, youth pastor, or favorite relative would talk with him or her. Your child will be waiting for the other shoe to drop, but bite your tongue and don't drop the shoe! Keep it warm and friendly. When you are finished, give your child a hug and tell him or her how much you enjoyed being together. Kids hang out with their friends, they hang out at malls, and they hang out at school. Since hanging out is one of their favorite pastimes, join in with them. You still have those twenty things on your agenda, don't you? So now, after some hang-out time, ask your child when would be a good time to go over some responsibilities or your agenda. You'll usually get a better reception.

Terri was one of those Type A moms who accomplished more in one day than I could in one week. She was so driven that her children and husband were beginning to find ways to avoid her. Her daughter complained to me that although her mom meant well, almost every night when she was tired and getting ready for bed, her mom would start with the twenty questions and school problems and whatever else was on her list. Usually the conversation would turn into a fight, with doors slamming and words spoken that they both later regretted.

The young girl told me, "My mom greets me at the door after school with a 'to do' list and doesn't give me a break until I go to sleep. Sometimes

I fake like I'm sleeping because I don't want Mom to ask me another question or challenge me with one more problem."

I knew Terri, so I understood she wasn't "the wicked witch of the west," but I concluded that perhaps she was developing an unhealthy parenting habit. My suggestion was for the mother not to greet her daughter with a "to do" list and definitely not to follow her around as she was getting ready for bed. Terri would be much better off if she greeted her daughter with warmth and affection and then made sure that the last event of the day centered on warmth and affection. However, the daughter needed to have daily, specific times when her homework would be checked and "the list" could be taken care of, so that Mom's agenda was handled and daughter felt the warmth and affection of a beautiful relationship.

If I were sitting with your child and spouse, how would they rate the "warmth" of your home? No one is looking for a fake sense of peace, but happy, healthy families work on creating a positive, warm environment even in the midst of needing to discipline and live out our daily lives.

ENCOURAGEMENT

Set realistic expectations. One of my spiritual gifts is the gift of exhortation or encouragement. I always thought that this gift only included being positive to people. But actually the gift of exhortation or encouragement means "to come alongside." When you encourage your children or your spouse, you have the unique ability to make them feel special. Your life and words speak into their lives with comfort, counsel, affirmation, and challenge. Exhortation is not just about positive reinforcement and encouragement; it is also about challenging our children to be all they were created to be by God.

You can encourage your children by setting realistic expectations for them. Many kids suffer from very poor self-images. They play the comparison game and lose every single time. When it comes to brains, beauty, and bucks, our society is not kind to this generation of young people. If we aren't careful, we as parents will reinforce the unreal expectations that our children are confronted with daily by our culture.

A couple came into my office very upset about their teenage daughter, who had decided to be influenced by the "punk rock" culture. Her hair was dyed stark white. Every piece of clothing she was wearing was black, and her makeup definitely made the statement "I don't want to be like my parents." Her mother and father were both successful business-people, dressed very conservatively. They looked professional and successful. Their daughter seemed nice enough, but even as a youth worker who had seen it all, I thought she looked, well, "Halloweenish." I thought, *I'm glad my daughters don't look like her.*

As the parents began to talk about their daughter, they were very tough on her, expressing some very lofty goals that she was never going to make—at least not in her current frame of mind. Her parents were both Stanford University graduates, and they expected their daughter to be getting straight As and following in their footsteps. They kept saying when she was younger she never received even one B, and she didn't understand that success was spelled Stanford, As, business, and a new hair style! In some ways as a parent I could understand their concerns, but I still felt uneasy. Their daughter was very polite the entire time as her parents unfolded their plan for her life. Now it was her turn.

The parents probably thought I asked a weird question. I turned to their daughter and asked, "So what excites you about life besides rock music?" She paused, smiled, and said, "Art."

"Art?" I repeated, surprised.

"Yeah, art. When I was little, Mom would take me to museums, and I fell in love with art. I love music, just not *their* kind. I love impressionistic painting. I love drama. I would like to work on Broadway as either an actor or artist."

To be honest, I didn't expect what I heard. I expected a caustic teenager, rebellious and self-centered. What I heard behind her purple eyeliner and bright red lipstick was a very articulate, well-educated, enthusiastic young lady with a passion for art and theater.

Now I had a dilemma. I didn't especially like her style of dress, but what she said made sense. She loved her parents but just didn't want to grow up to be them. She had a flair for the artistic side of life, and they had a flair for business. Her parents wanted her to have a Stanford business degree with straight As, but she wanted to go to a college that had a wonderful performing arts program and study her own interests. They needed some good old-fashioned compromise and negotiation. If her parents continued to force business and Stanford on her, they were setting themselves up for a colossal failure. If she totally rebelled against her parents' values and relationship, she would be flirting with disaster.

We took out a blank piece of paper. The parents and daughter negotiated a new set of expectations: "We will drop our expectation of a Stanford business degree if you will go to class, do your homework, and try your best to get into the school of your choice." "We'll quit nagging you about your clothing under the condition that you wear something besides black every day." Before the meeting was over, they had a new set of expectations in writing that both parents and daughter could live with and dialogue about. Their daughter was not an "A" student, but she wasn't a dropout either.

The question in my mind when they left my office was, "Will these parents be able to encourage their daughter to excel with her interests?"

The answer is that they absolutely did encourage her. They call that meeting their "parenting conversion." Today, their daughter is a vibrant, talented, young actress with a deep Christian commitment. She threw away her punk rock outfits but still doesn't own a business suit.

Whether your child is four, eleven, or sixteen, what are your expectations for them that may not be appropriate? What expectations are mutually acceptable, healthy, and worthy of your time and energy? Don't forget to set the bar for success for your kids. Every child isn't an "A" student, and they won't all be captain of the team or get the lead in the play. However, every child needs to know he or she is loved and believed in. Don't fight every battle, only the absolutely necessary ones. Encouragement means coming alongside our children and helping them be all God created them to be.

At the beginning of this chapter, I shared about my friend Rob Thibaut. Rob, one of the most wonderful people I have ever known, was a Harvard MBA business guy. One day I learned a very valuable lesson from him. His grown daughter lived in a different state, and they talked regularly on the phone. He told me that he always had an agenda with his daughter. He would say hi and then get into his agenda. One day he called her and didn't go through any agenda. They talked about a ski trip his daughter had taken. They talked about boys and the weather and a TV program. After twenty minutes he told Angela he loved her and said good-bye. She called him back ten minutes later and said, "I just called to say thanks for taking the time out of your busy schedule to call me. I love you." She responded to his genuine interest and care.

I asked Rob, "So when did you get through your list for Angela?"

He smiled and said, "I got two of my main issues dealt with on her return phone call!"

So what's the point? Deal with the issues of the family by creating times of affection, warmth, and encouragement first, and then your children may be more receptive to doing "family business."

FURTHER READING

- Smalley, Gary, and John Trent. *The Blessing*. Nashville: Thomas Nelson, 1986.

  For more information on parenting with A.W.E. (affirmation, warmth, encouragement), articles, information, and discussions, check out youthbuilders.com. It's filled with hundreds of practical helps for parents, students, and youth workers.

DISCUSSION STARTERS

1. Did you grow up in a family with an emphasis toward shame-based parenting or A.W.E.–based parenting? How did it affect you?

2. What specific steps can you take to enhance an environment of A.W.E. in your family? What makes it difficult?

3. "Every child needs someone who is irrationally positive about them." Did you have that person in your life? Who is or can become that person in the lives of your children?

4. Read the following scriptures, keeping in mind that both Cephas (Aramaic) and Petras (Greek) mean "the rock":

And he [Andrew] brought him [Simon] to Jesus. Jesus looked at him and said, "You are Simon son of John. You will be called Cephas" (which, when translated, is Peter). (John 1:42)

And I tell you that you are Peter, and on this rock I will build my church, and the gates of Hades will not overcome it. (Matt. 16:18)

Jesus had the power to believe in the bigmouthed fisherman, and he became the leader of the early church. What can you do to believe in your child more? Who is the "Simon Peter" in your life right now?

3

BUILD HEALTHY MORALS AND VALUES

At one point during the game, the coach said to one of his young play-
ers, "Do you understand what cooperation is and what teamwork is
all about?" The little boy nodded in the affirmative.

"Do you understand that what really matters is not whether we
win or lose, but that we play together as a team?" The little boy nod-
ded yes.

"Good," the coach continued. "And, when a strike is called, or
you're thrown out at first, you don't argue, curse, attack the umpire
with a bat, or throw dirt in the opposing team member's face. Do you
understand all that?" Again the little boy nodded. "Well sure, coach.
That's what you taught us."

"Good," said the coach. "Now, please go over there and explain all
that to your mother!"

I LOOKED OUT AT AN AUDIENCE of sixteen-year-old students and
began my talk by making this statement: "I'm very glad I'm not sixteen
years old right now. It's more difficult to grow up today than it was way
back when I was sixteen." Let's face it, as parents we were once four years
of age and eight and eleven and sixteen, but we were *never* their age
because today's children experience so much so young.

Sure, we had to deal with peer pressure and sexual temptations. Your parents probably griped to you about your choice of music and your choice of language. Students took drugs in your day, and most young boys sneaked a look at a *Playboy*. However, we were still *never* their age. Today's child or teenager can type in one word on the Internet and be exposed to more blatant pornography than you even thought existed back in the good old days.

Someone recently told me that the average junior higher is exposed to more sexually explicit innuendos on the way to and from school than he was during his entire teenage years. My friend may be right! The average young person can watch more than fourteen thousand acts of intercourse or innuendo on prime-time TV each year, and the media is getting more brazen and extreme in every avenue of exposure. On average, the first taste of alcohol happened at age fifteen for the previous generation; today it is age twelve.

There's no doubt about it: Being a kid today is much more difficult than it was when we were their age. This means that producing a happy, healthy family takes more proactive work on the parents' part than ever before. At the same time, we have fewer extended family support systems in place and less free time to be proactive about providing healthy moral guidance and values for our family. Far too many parents subsidize their God-given responsibility of teaching morals and values to their kids by allowing the schools, TV, or even the church to be their children's primary teacher.

However, the biblical mandate all the way back to the days of Moses was that the primary responsibility of teaching and training children was handed down from God to the parents. "These commandments that I give you today are to be upon your hearts. Impress them on your children. Talk about them when you sit at home and when you walk along the road, when you lie down and when you get up" (Deut. 6:6–7).

Here's part of the problem. Most of us parents didn't receive positive, healthy, value-centered education from home. Our parents may have tried, but their parents didn't do the job either, so the cycle continues until today. Only 10 to 15 percent of adolescents tell us that they receive any kind of good, positive, healthy, value-centered sex education or drug education from home.

MIXED MESSAGES

Kids are receiving mixed messages when it comes to morals and values. Let's take sexuality for example. From home they hear, "Don't do *it*" but not much more about the subject. From church (although it is hopefully changing for the better), they often hear either silence or, "Don't do *it* because *it's* dirty, rotten, and ugly." From the secular media they often hear, "Do *it*." The secular media is thrilled to sing, write, and make movies about sexual promiscuity. Kids today are much more influenced when it comes to issues like drugs, sex, and rock-'n'-roll from the secular media than from their mom and dad. It's time to bring it back home when it comes to teaching our children about morals and values. Morals and values education belongs first and foremost in the home.

Kids today are making decisions about sex, drugs, and music based on at least three reasons that parents must be aware of and be prepared to respond to in a proactive manner.

Peer pressure. Peer pressure is one of the most powerful forces among kids of all ages. If your children's friends experiment with marijuana or pornography, then the odds are great that your children will too. The first time I took a sip of alcohol I was thirteen. I was at a party where there was alcohol, and though I had already decided I would not drink, my desire to be accepted by my friends was much greater than my desire not to drink.

Emotional involvement that exceeds their maturity level. Kids are making decisions based on emotional involvement that exceed their maturity level. For example, a fourteen-year-old girl with a poor self-image who is "in love" with a sexually promiscuous older guy unfortunately becomes easy to seduce. Her emotional involvement and desire to be liked by the guy is far stronger than the morals she may have learned from home, church, or school. So she gives in to temptation, not because she's a bad kid, but simply because no one ever helped her learn how to say no. If you have a late bloomer in your home, then get down on your knees and thank God. The decisions kids are making about morals and values today can and do affect them for life. Just in case you think that dating at an early age is OK, look at these facts:

AGE OF DATING	% WHO HAVE SEX BEFORE GRADUATION
12 Years	91%
13 Years	56%
14 Years	53%
15 Years	40%
16 Years	20%

Lack of information. Kids are making moral decisions based simply on a lack of information. All studies (both from conservatives and liberals) point out that the more positive, value-centered sex education kids receive, the less promiscuous they will be. The same goes for drug and alcohol education and for all values-type education. The United States government has finally admitted that abstinence education is the most effective way to teach sex education in the public schools and has recently released millions of dollars to fund abstinence education in classrooms because it's the only type of education that has produced positive results.

Parents, we must become students of the culture and take responsibility for equipping our children to develop sound biblical values and morals that will keep them from the dangerous influences of our culture. It isn't an easy job for parents. We are bound to face some bumps, bruises, and missed opportunities along the way. But take the time to learn from the experts on the subject of morals and values. Start with your young children and keep working on the family values as your children move toward independence in the later teen and young adult years.

Every six months or so, Cathy and I plan a day away from our normal schedule and take an extended time to focus on each of our children. We try to make a fun day out of it with a nice lunch or a day at the beach with our pens and notebooks. We examine the areas of our children's lives that we believe are crucial for us as parents to be very present in, and we discuss, make plans, and create an agenda for each child for the coming six months. During this day, we talk about what we hope to teach each child in the areas of morals and values, school issues, relationships, friendships, health issues, and especially spiritual growth. Many times Cathy and I have disagreed over a parenting position, but our parenting retreats are always time well invested, and they have definitely made us better, more proactive parents. We close our time praying for each child and for us to be parents who will remain strong with our biblical convictions on parenting at this time in our lives, with three strong-willed adolescent girls.

We've made important decisions during these times, such as our decision to take our youngest away for the "mom-and-daughter sex talk" an entire year earlier than the other two girls and to do more family fun days in the next six months. Cathy and I both feel that our focused time away is a must for healthy parenting. Otherwise life gets too busy and complicated. That's when we allow circumstances and chance to take the place of proactive parenting.

Although this book is not meant to be the end-all on morals and values, I want to take a look at several of the big issues, along with some practical action steps to take.

SEX AND SEXUALITY

Your children deserve honest, open, blunt, and unashamedly biblical answers in the area of sex and sexuality. Obviously, your input with your children must be age-appropriate and consistent. Cathy and I like to go back to the list we make every six months and then look for informal times and teachable moments to bring in the truths we hope to get across.

Remember to be age-appropriate. Books on child development and sex education will help you figure out what to talk about at what age. Don't be like the mother who was greeted by her seven-year-old son one day after school with, "Mom, what is sex?" The mother was shocked that the question came when he was still so young. *Where is my husband when I need him?* she thought.

Mom decided to face her fear and just go ahead and tell him everything. She pulled out a plate of cookies and a glass of milk and proceeded to give her son "the sex talk." She drew pictures. She gave proper names and functions of each intimate aspect of sex. Her son didn't say a word but listened intently with his eyes as big as saucers while finishing off all the cookies. Finally after a very intense forty-five minutes, the mother asked, "Son, do you have any questions?"

"Yeah, Mom, just one. I still don't know what I am supposed to write on my soccer form where it says 'Sex: Please circle M or F.'" He wasn't ready for the whole story; he just wanted to understand what he was supposed to write on the application!

Here's the list Cathy and I created of things we want to talk about with our daughters relating to sex, dating, and sexuality. Keep in mind that sex education starts early and continues with age-appropriate disclosure through adolescence.

- Appropriate touch and nonappropriate touch
- What the Bible says about sex and sexuality
- Definition of puberty
- Changes in hair and body, including body size and shape
- Menstrual periods
- Sexual organs
- Emotions
- Sexual attraction
- Infatuation versus real love
- Masturbation
- Pornography
- Sexual abuse, harassment, and teasing
- Sexual intercourse
- Virginity
- Why wait
- Pregnancy
- Dangers of sexual relationships
- Partying
- The cultural influence of sex and sexuality
- Abstinence and purity
- How far is too far?
- Dating
- Homosexuality
- AIDS

MEDIA

Media is not neutral in our lives. It has slowly invaded almost every aspect of our world. In fact, American children spend more time watching television than any other activity of their waking lives. The retention level for reading this book or listening to a speech is about 5 to 10 percent retention. However, the retention level of televised media is more than 25 percent recall. This means whatever your children put into their minds via TV and movies is stored in the computer of their brain.

Parents must take a proactive approach to what enters their children's lives via media. Today we are fortunate because we do have books, periodicals, and the Web to help us learn more about the latest media influence. You can get reviews of movies or the words of the popular songs your children are being influenced by, as well as the latest information on TV programming. The following "tips to tame the tube" have helped our family greatly and in all honesty almost caused a few riots with a couple of the Burns teenagers! However, it has been our guide and a good one at that.

TIPS TO TAME THE TUBE

The TV is not a baby-sitter. Hopefully, parents are extremely careful about choosing a baby-sitter and day care for their children. Why are we not as careful about choosing the programs our children watch on TV?

Know what shows your kids are watching on TV. It is vitally important to know the content of every program your child watches. For younger children, videos are much easier to monitor. Ask the question, "Is the content in line with our moral guidelines?" If TV is not working to enhance your values, it may just be working to oppose your values with a much higher budget than you have. Throw away the remote, or at least save it only when Dad *must* watch two football games at the same time!

Don't put a TV in your child's bedroom. A TV in your child's bedroom is a big no-no. You won't be able to monitor the content, and your kids will be drawn to their rooms at the expense of family interaction. A TV in the bedroom is a far too attractive temptation that easily interrupts such important matters as sleep, schoolwork, reading, and interaction with others.

Set limits on TV time. What are your guidelines, rules, and expectations for TV viewing? Can your children watch TV before school? How about before homework is finished? How many hours a day can the TV be on? Setting limits may be a challenge to your whole family, but with consistency the results are well worth it.

Make an appointment with the TV. It's a good idea to be proactive about your TV use and misuse. Many healthy families pull out the TV guide on a weekly basis and make TV appointments for the week. This monitors how often and what shows your family is watching and can make a TV program a family activity. Not too much butter on the popcorn though! Mom and Dad, why don't you make appointments with the TV also? Children see; children do.

Dialogue with your children about TV shows. All television is educational. The question is, What does it teach? Recently, I gave in to a movie on TV under the condition that afterward we would discuss it and react to it. The movie wasn't as gross as I thought it would be, but together we debriefed the themes and content over frozen yogurt and turned a mediocre movie into a first-rate learning experience.

The VCR can be your friend. If you can't watch the few good shows on

TV because of your family's schedule, then tape them and watch them as a family. Make the VCR your friend.

INTERNET

The World Wide Web is here to stay. The Internet is one of those once-in-a-decade revolutionary developments that will change many aspects of everyday life. To put the Net in context, here are the most significant technological developments of the past five decades:

> 1950s Television
> 1960s Mainframe computer
> 1970s Electronic chip
> 1980s Personal computer
> 1990s Internet

It's important to remember that each of these developments contributed to a vast array of changes that affected almost every aspect of life. However, of the five, the Internet will turn out to be the most important development, the one that will change your children's lives in more ways than the other four. So fasten your seat belt and brace yourself for the ride of your life. This is the era of the Internet, and the Internet will have more influence on your family quite possibly than the television did on your parents' homes.

Your children are growing up with one of the most incredible tools ever invented right in front of them. Generally speaking, people twenty-four and older use the Internet as a tool, but people under twenty-four use it as a way of life.

Whether you are Web savvy today doesn't matter, but by tomorrow you had better be on your way to becoming an expert. Just because my eighty-two-year-old dad doesn't trust an ATM machine doesn't mean that his children don't use them. When radio first came on to the scene, one famous pastor said, "This will never last." Well, the World Wide Web is here to stay, and your children's lives will be changed forever because of it.

The Web is wonderful, but the Web is dangerous. So learn all you can about the Web and make it your friend. Just like friends at school, it will either be a positive influence on your children or a negative one. There has never been a time when the world had a greater access to positive information and negative influences. For example, there are an estimated one hundred thousand Internet pornography sites, and that number is growing by two hundred sites every day.[1] I'm glad I'm not a twelve-year-old boy anymore tempted by the call of the darker side of the Web.

In the name of practicality, there are several steps you can take to help ensure that the Web is your friend:

Consider a quality Web filter for young children and young teens. This isn't the only answer, but it is a good start. (You can get many good ideas for Web filters by looking at the parents' section of <u>youthbuilders.com.</u>)

Keep the computer with on-line access out of your child's room or any back room that might be out of the way of people traffic. Know which Web sites your child is viewing and interacting in.

Remind your child not to give out personal information over the Web without your permission. Unfortunately, there are some very sick people out there, and they love the privacy of the Web. You would do better if your kids were only on "approved by Mom and Dad" chat rooms if you allow chat rooms at all.

Teach your kids that if someone offensive interacts with them on-line they should report it to you right away. Sexual abusers and predators lurk in some incredibly unique places. Don't hesitate to report any, and I mean any, questionable Internet activity to the local authorities. Didn't someone once say, "It's better to be safe than sorry"? As a parent, you're in the protection business.

MUSIC

Another one of the greatest influences in your child's life will be the music they listen to. Don't buy the story that your children don't listen to the words. Music and musicians have a great deal of influence on our culture. MTV is not a music channel; it's a youth culture. I would suggest you develop a music and media-viewing contract with your children at a young age. Learn what's influencing them in these very vulnerable years.

With our teenagers, Cathy and I have a policy that we listen to all CDs brought into the house. Sure it takes a great deal of time listening to some styles of music that aren't our favorite, but we must become students of the youth culture. We believe we have a God-given responsibility to review and, yes, even approve what words our children listen to in our home.

The Music Agreement
Hours music can be on in the home _____
Any groups or music not allowed in the home _____
Concerts your children may or may not attend _____

TV/Movie-Viewing Contract

The average amount of hours the TV can be on in our home per day is

_____

The movie ratings that are available for each family member to view are

_____

The TV programs that are not acceptable in our home are

_____

The family agreement about MTV is

_____

A TV program that could be a fun family weekly date is

_____

A movie that fits biblical standards that we can watch as a family is

_____

DRUGS AND ALCOHOL

When Steve Arterburn and I wrote the book *Drug-Proof Your Kids,* we were amazed at two statistics that kept popping up in our research. Ninety-two percent of all pastors said there was a problem with drugs and alcohol in their community, but only 13 percent thought there was a problem with drugs and alcohol in their churches. Incidentally, Christian parents believed the same. The second troubling statistic was that there was only about a 5 to 10 percent difference in use and abuse of drugs and alcohol between kids who attend church and kids who don't. There has never been a time when children were more susceptible to drug and alcohol abuse, and yet, without trying to offend you, most parents are either in denial or ignorant of the issues of drug and alcohol abuse until it is too late. Parents of happy, healthy families study the threat of drug and alcohol abuse and teach their children about the dangers.

I choose not to drink for three reasons: Christy Meredith Burns, Rebecca Joy Burns, and Heidi Michelle Burns. I believe there is a biological predisposition toward alcoholism passed on from generation to generation. I have alcoholism on both sides of my family tree, so I choose not to drink just in case it's in my system and in their genes. If they see Dad drink, then they may justify their own drinking because of Dad. And since alcoholism is in our family's genes, their bodies may crave alcohol differently than others.[2]

Gateway drugs. All parents should help their kids from a young age understand what are called "gateway drugs." Here's how they work. Kids begin their experimentation with beer and wine. That's usually where substance abuse begins and, as I mentioned before, today the average first drink happens around twelve years old. The majority of kids will try alcohol before they graduate from high school. If kids do try beer and wine, they have a greater chance of moving through the gateway to nicotine.

Nicotine. The tobacco industry has done a pitiful job of keeping future underage addicts from experimenting. But is it really the tobacco industry's fault, or should the blame equally fall on us parents who haven't taught our kids about the harmful effects of the very strong drug called nicotine? Did you know that it's actually easier to get off of heroin than nicotine? The detoxification period of heroin is terrible, but after about five days the drug has passed through the user's system. With the intense addiction to nicotine, some say it is nearly impossible to shake the habit. The fact is that 81 percent of kids who smoke cigarettes will move farther through the gateway to experiment with marijuana. Yet only 20 percent of the kids who do not smoke will ever try marijuana.

Harder alcohol. First of all, let's get something straight: Alcohol is a drug. It's a drug because it is mood- and mind-altering. It is also a poison. Why? Because it's toxic. Most teenagers, and especially college students, know someone who has died or become extremely sick from putting too much alcohol into their body.

Because our family has alcoholism all over our family tree, we have had to teach our kids about this frightening disease. All alcoholics have a high tolerance for alcohol and can consume a great amount of alcohol without it affecting them like a nonalcoholic. In fact, many budding alcoholics consume a great amount of alcohol, yet since they drink below their tolerance level, they are praised for being able to hold their liquor. I know a sixteen-year-old young man who proudly told me he could drink five beers and not get drunk. He was surprised at my answer. I told him, "I believe you and, in fact, I would rather have you as the designated driver than someone who is slushy drunk on two beers." Then I went for the jugular. I bluntly said, "You must be a budding alcoholic."

Surprised, he protested, "Maybe you didn't understand. I'm not even drunk after five beers."

I said, "I understand perfectly. Your body has a high tolerance for alcohol. The problem is, like all alcoholics, your body craves alcohol differently than nonalcoholics and will begin to break down. And unless you quit drinking, you will live a life very similar to your dad's." He had already told me that he had little respect for his father, who was a drunk and had left the family for his secretary. His father's alcoholism had messed up his life as well as taken a toll on the whole family.

Marijuana. Marijuana is a similar step through the gateway as alcohol. When I graduated from Anaheim High School in 1971, we were told that marijuana was not harmful to our health. Hardly anyone is saying that today. We still don't know everything about this popular drug, but we do know that in many people it produces a sickness called "amotivational syndrome." Amotivational syndrome is when your brain becomes lazy and lethargic. Most of us have a friend or two who smoked just a bit too much pot, and although they function, they are just sloooow.

The other important factor for parents to know is that the marijuana that Bill Clinton and others did not inhale in the 1970s is not the same marijuana drug as kids are using today. Today's marijuana is five to twenty times stronger and is often laced with more dangerous drugs.

Heroin, LSD, cocaine. Then we move on to heroin, LSD, and cocaine. Your children likely won't start their experimentation with these drugs, but as kids move through the gateway, they find it easier to violate their value systems and move to harder drugs. Each step further through the gateway brings people closer to hard-core drugs and more destruction.

Healthy parental drug education is an answer. The chances of drug abuse in a young person's life go down when parents proactively teach their kids and set a good example themselves. The first step in preventing drug and alcohol abuse with your kids is self-examination. I know one father who tried to get help for his two sons for several years. On the day he admitted he had a problem with alcohol, his sons followed him to treatment.

Most likely every parent reading this book has made the decision to strengthen and teach his or her children positive, healthy morals and values. Most parents are frightened by the amount of negative distractions and temptations facing today's children. However, if they are given proper education, a good example, positive faith, and proactive parenting, your children can make it through the maze of the negative influences and develop positive morals and values that they will pass on to their children.

FURTHER READING

- Arterburn, Stephen, and Jim Burns. *Parent's Guide to the Top Ten Dangers Teens Face.* Colorado Springs: Focus on the Family, 1995.

- McDowell, Josh. *The Disconnected Generation: Saving Our Youth from Self-Destruction.* Nashville: Word, 2000.

- McDowell, Josh. *Right from Wrong.* Nashville: Word, 1994.

- Rainey, Dennis, and Barbara Rainey. *Parenting Today's Adolescent: Helping Your Child Avoid the Traps of the Preteen and Early Teen Years.* Nashville: Thomas Nelson, 1998.

DISCUSSION STARTERS

1. Where did you receive most of your influential morals and values when you were a child?

2. What are your fears for your own children about today's moral decay of the world?

3. What positive steps are you taking to protect and help your children fight the negative values of our day?

4. What positive suggestions were most helpful in this chapter?

5. How does the following passage relate to training our children to have biblical morals and values?

Train a child in the way he should go, and when he is old he will not turn from it. (Prov. 22:6)

If you suspect that you have a child or a family member with a drug or alcohol problem, seek help immediately. Here's a helpful parent questionnaire to use when you suspect that someone you know and love may have a problem in this area.

QUESTIONS FOR PARENTS ON ALCOHOLISM AND DRUG USE AND ABUSE

You may suspect that your child or teenager is having trouble with alcohol and other drugs, but short of smelling liquor on his breath or discovering pills in her pockets, how can you tell for sure? While symptoms vary, there are some common tip-offs. Your answers to the following questions will help you determine if a problem exists:

1. Has your child's personality changed markedly? Does he or she change moods quickly, seem sullen, withdraw from the family, display sudden anger or depression, or spend hours alone in his or her room?

   Yes _____ No _____ Uncertain _____

2. Has your child lost interest in school, school activities, or school athletics? Have his or her grades dropped at all?

   Yes _____ No _____ Uncertain _____

3. Has your child stopped spending time with old friends? Is he or she now spending time with kids who worry

you? Is your child secretive or evasive about his or her friends, where they go, and what they do?

Yes _____ No _____ Uncertain _____

4. Are you missing money or other objects from around the house (money needed for alcohol and drugs), or have you noticed that your child has more money than you would expect (possibly from selling drugs)?

Yes _____ No _____ Uncertain _____

5. Has your child been involved with the law in a situation involving drugs in any way? (You can be assured that if this has happened, there have been other times—probably many—when he or she has been drinking or using drugs but hasn't gotten caught.)

Yes _____ No _____ Uncertain _____

6. Does your child get angry and defensive when you talk to him or her about alcohol and drugs or refuse to discuss the topic at all? (People who are very defensive about alcohol and drugs are often hiding how much they use.)

Yes _____ No _____ Uncertain _____

7. Has your child become dishonest? Do you feel you're not getting straight answers about your child's whereabouts, activities, or companions? A young person may also lie about matters that seem unrelated to alcohol or drugs.

Yes _____ No _____ Uncertain _____

8. Are there physical signs of alcohol or drug use? Have you smelled alcohol on your child's breath? Have you smelled the odor of marijuana on his or her clothing or in his or her room? Slurred speech, unclear thinking, or swaggering gait are also indicators. Bloodshot eyes, dilated pupils, and imprecise eye movement may also be clues.

Yes _____ No _____ Uncertain _____

9. Has your child lost interest in previously important hobbies, sports, or other activities? Has your child lost motivation, enthusiasm, and vitality?

Yes _____ No _____ Uncertain _____

10. Have you seen evidence of alcohol or drugs? Have you ever found a hidden bottle, beer cans left in the car, marijuana seeds, marijuana cigarettes, cigarette rolling papers, drug paraphernalia (pipes, roach clips, stash cans, etc.), capsules, or tablets?

Yes _____ No _____ Uncertain _____

11. Has your child's relationship with you or other family members deteriorated? Does your child avoid family gatherings? Is your child less interested in siblings, or does he or she now verbally (or even physically) abuse younger brothers and sisters?

Yes _____ No _____ Uncertain _____

12. Has your child ever been caught with alcohol or drugs at school or school activities?

Yes _____ No _____ Uncertain _____

13. Has your child seemed sick, fatigued, or grumpy (possibly hung over) in the morning after drug or alcohol use was possible the night before?

Yes _____ No _____ Uncertain _____

14. Has your child's grooming deteriorated? Does your child dress in a way that is associated with drug or alcohol use? Does your child seem unusually interested in drug or alcohol-related slogans, posters, music, or clothes?

Yes _____ No _____ Uncertain _____

15. Has your child's physical appearance changed? Does he or she appear unhealthy, lethargic, more forgetful, or have a shorter attention span than before?

Yes _____ No _____ Uncertain _____

How to Score the Test

This questionnaire is not a scientific instrument and is not meant to diagnose alcohol and drug problems. It is meant to alert parents that problems are likely. The questions are "red flag" detectors, and your answers may show a need for further action. Keep in mind that "yes" answers to some of these questions may simply reflect normal adolescent behavior. "Yes" answers to questions directly relating to alcohol and drug use (5, 8, 10, 12) are, of course, cause for concern; they indicate that your child is using alcohol and/or drugs, and action should be taken.

In general, parents should look for an emerging pattern. A couple of "yes" or "uncertain" answers should alert parents to suspect alcohol and drug use, monitor the child more closely, talk to knowledgeable sources, and prepare to seek help.

If you answered "yes" to three or more questions, you probably need to seek help. Your child may be in the experimental stages or may already be heavily involved in alcohol and drugs. Remember, it is very, very difficult to handle this problem without the help of other experienced parents and/or professionals. This is not often a problem that passes with time; it may well be a life-or-death matter. If you are concerned, take action: Call a knowledgeable source, your school counselor, or other alcoholism/drug counselors who deal with adolescents, your local council on alcoholism, or another drug/alcohol agency and discuss this questionnaire.

4

DISCIPLINE WITH CONSISTENCY

We tried so hard to make things better for our kids that we made them worse. For my grandchildren, I'd like better. I'd really like for them to know about hand-me-down clothes and homemade ice cream and leftover meatloaf sandwiches. I really would. I hope you learn humility by being humiliated and that you learn honesty by being cheated. I hope you learn to make your bed, mow the lawn, and wash the car. And I really hope nobody gives you a brand-new car when you are sixteen. It will be good if at least one time you can see puppies born and your old dog put to sleep.

I hope you get a black eye fighting for something you believe in. I hope you have to share a bedroom with your younger brother. And it's all right if you have to draw a line down the middle of the room, but when he wants to crawl under the covers with you because he's scared, I hope you let him. When you want to see a movie and your little sister wants to tag along, I hope you'll let her.

I hope you have to walk uphill to school with your friends and that you live in a town where you can do it safely. On rainy days when you have to catch a ride, I hope you don't ask your "driver" to drop you two blocks away so you won't be seen riding with someone as uncool as your mom.

If you want a slingshot, I hope your dad teaches you how to make one instead of buying one. I hope you learn to dig in the dirt and read books. When you learn to use computers, I hope you also learn how to add and subtract in your head. I hope you get teased by your friends when you have your first crush on a girl and when you talk back to your mother that you learn what Ivory soap tastes like.

May you skin your knee climbing a mountain, burn your hand on a stove, and stick your tongue on a frozen flagpole. I sure hope you make time to sit on a porch with your grandma and go fishing with your uncle.

May you feel sorrow at a funeral and joy during the holidays. I hope your mother punishes you when you throw a baseball through a neighbor's window and that she hugs you and kisses you at Christmastime when you give her a mold of your hand. These things I wish for you—tough times and disappointments, hard work and happiness. To me, it's the only way to appreciate life.[1]

WHEN OUR OLDEST DAUGHTER, Christy, was thirteen years old, we had a special meeting with her and told her we would buy her a car on her eighteenth birthday under the condition that she stayed drug- and alcohol-free during her teenage years. We didn't promise a nice car, and at thirteen she didn't really care about the kind of car. We promised that it would have four wheels and an engine that worked. About six months later we added sexual promiscuity to the contract. I don't think Christy remembers that the sexual abstinence part was an add-on! I'm not even sure if Christy has been tempted much in the world of drugs and sex. She is a pretty exceptional kid. I do know that she tells her friends about our contract and that she wears a sexual purity pledge ring as a covenant she made with God, her future spouse, and her parents.

When I mention this particular contract idea on radio or in seminars, I get mixed reactions. Some parents don't like the idea at all, and others take their children out to dinner that night to do the same thing. Some look at it as bribing and others brilliance. Only time will tell. The problem with developing contracts with our children is that each child responds to different kinds of boundaries in different ways. Cathy and I find that what works perfectly for Christy doesn't work with our other two daughters, Rebecca and Heidi. When Heidi was little, all we had to do was give her *the look* and she basically disciplined herself. Rebecca, who can have her father's stubborn streak, needed to be threatened with a "lifetime of grounding," and then it was very important that we stick with our word.

Happy, healthy families set expressed expectations with positive limits, boundaries, and consistent discipline. Rebecca had been begging us for a dog for years. Cathy was willing, but I had put my foot down. "No dogs when the kids don't feed, clean, or pay attention to the cats we already have." It was Christmastime, and Cathy found a beautiful golden retriever puppy that would be ready to arrive in a home on Christmas Day. I asked, "Who will groom the dog, feed the dog, scoop up after the dog, take the dog to the vet, and walk the dog?" "Of course, the girls will," was Cathy's reply. Well, the dog was cute and I knew it would please Rebecca and all the girls. So in a weak moment I said yes. (Life is not easy for a male with all females in the house, a common theme in my life.)

We picked up the dog late Christmas Eve with our friend Pam. What would we do with the dog until Christmas morning? I was already having second and third thoughts. Pam offered to stay at our house so I could sleep with the dog at hers. *Great,* I thought. It was Christmas Eve, and I was relegated to a vacant home with a puppy that stayed up most of the night and kept messing on Pam's rug, which I cleaned twice: at 3:20 A.M. and 4:45 A.M. When I arrived home blurry eyed and beat up by the events of the predawn dog episode, the girls saw the puppy and were ecstatic. We named him Hobie, after the surfboard. All was well until we realized someone would have to clean the messes and train this puppy that had a passion for chewing shoes, curtains, and wood tables. For some reason, I was elected to train the puppy to be just like our neighbor Bill's dog, the perfect one.

I asked my neighbor, "Bill, how did you train Molly to be such an obedient dog?"

"Oh, it's simple," he replied. "Take Hobie to doggy obedience school and then work with him daily for at least twenty to forty minutes." Oh great! I was looking for a much quicker and easier answer.

So the girls wished me luck as I picked up Hobie and literally carried him into his first day of puppy obedience school. When I got out of the car, I could see that Hobie was the rowdiest dog of the bunch, and furthermore, I wasn't sure if I was happy or embarrassed that the puppy trainer was a member of our church who was now very enthusiastically telling everyone about my work with youth and families. Just great. The "family expert" had the worst-behaving dog in the entire group.

Our instructor said, "Today we will not work with your dogs." I was disappointed; I had hoped that by the end of the first class Hobie would be fully trained. Our instructor continued, "Most of puppy training isn't really training the dog; that's the easiest part. Most of the training will be for you, the happy dog owners. Excellent dog training is at least two-thirds training the humans; the easiest part is working with the dogs." Then he shared the kicker. "I want to share with you three statements right from the beginning that I actually learned from Jim, the man over there with the hyperactive golden retriever, when he and his wife taught a parenting class at our church." (I knew I was in trouble when all the other "happy dog owners" looked at me, and my puppy was the only one that had twisted the leash around my legs so I couldn't move.) I just smiled and regretted at that moment teaching the class and bringing home the puppy for Christmas.

He continued, "As Jim over there says, show lots of love and affection to your dog, discipline with consistency, set limits and boundaries, and express your expectations clearly to your dogs." Oh great. I was having enough trouble following my own advice with my children, let alone this dog that had not stopped licking my shoes since the class began.

I'm happy to say Hobie passed the class. He is definitely *my* dog. And my instructor was right; I needed the training and obedience lessons more than the dog. The skills Hobie and I learned really were similar to child rearing. I needed to discipline with consistency in order for Hobie to not be an embarrassment to the entire neighborhood. Especially to Molly next door.

Not unlike dog training, parents need more help with discipline than the kids. Proper discipline is two-thirds parent training and one-third kid training. Disciplining my children consistently is the most difficult part of being a parent. We establish the rules, we set the boundaries, and then we allow the rules to be broken. Usually on days when I need to be liked or I'm too tired to do what is right, I realize too late that I have been manipulated by a person with one-third my age and experience. Healthy parenting takes time, energy, and work. As James Dobson said, "There is no assignment on earth that requires the array of skills and understanding needed by a mom in fulfilling her everyday duties."[2] Dobson was absolutely right when he said this about mothers, and I'm sure he would have included fathers also.

As I have said, if you are having an easy time as a parent, something is definitely wrong. Quality parenting is the most important legacy you will leave in this world, but nobody said it would be easy. Your job is to help them grow up to be responsible adults, not to be their best friend. That will come much later.

DISCIPLINE WITH CONSISTENCY

Discipline is a training process for the kids and for the parents. If you are married, you and your spouse will need to make a combined effort to figure out your strategy and then stick with it. If you are a single parent, you will need the help and influence of others who can support you to stick with being consistent with your discipline. For those who persevere there is a great promise from the Book of Proverbs: "Train a child in the way he should go, and when he is old he will not turn from it" (22:6). Keep that promise in mind at all times when you are sticking to your strategy.

The purpose of parental discipline is to teach responsibility rather than to evoke obedience. There are many toxic ways to manipulate obedience, but if you use them, you will lose in the long run. Our goal as parents is to move from control to influence. As children move from dependence toward independence, a healthy parenting plan will move from extreme control toward influence. You can't be your child's best friend *and* be the person who enforces boundaries and limits. At each stage of development, your child needs something different from you when it comes to control, influence, and discipline; but what your child needs most is consistency. The vast majority of kids in crisis I talk with tell me that they do not clearly understand their family limits and expressed expectations. Usually it's not the kids' fault, but rather the parents are throwing out too many mixed messages. Although the author is unknown, a very wise mother wrote these words:

"You don't love me!" How many times have your kids laid that one on you? And how many times have you, as a parent, resisted the urge to tell them how much?

Someday, when my children are old enough to understand the logic that motivates a mother, I'll tell them.

I love you enough to bug you about where you were going, with whom, and what time you would get home.

I loved you enough to be silent and let you discover your hand-picked friend was a creep.

I loved you enough to make you return a Milky Way with a bite out of it to a drugstore and confess, "I stole this."

I love you enough to stand over you for two hours while you cleaned your bedroom, a job that would have taken me fifteen minutes.

I loved you enough to not make excuses for your lack of respect or your bad manners.

I love you enough to ignore "what the other mother" did.

I loved you enough to figure you would lie about the party chaperone but forgive you for it . . . after discovering I was right.

I loved you enough to let you stumble, fall and fail so that you could learn to stand alone.

I loved you enough to accept you for what you are, and not what I wanted you to be.

But most of all, I loved you enough to say no when you hated me for it. That was the hardest part of all.

CHOICES AND CONSEQUENCES

Good parenting involves training our children in the areas of choices and consequences. Most of life involves choices and consequences. If you make wise choices, usually the consequences are positive. If you make poor choices, then negative consequences will ultimately follow. Some parents are a bit too rigid with choices and consequences, but by far most of us struggle with being consistent. We have opinions about movies, music, friendships, talking back, curfew, lying, and hundreds of other issues, but because of our own humanity and an incredible need to be liked, we often miss the mark and are inconsistent when it comes to teaching our children that there are consequences for most every action they choose. Not only is it true while your children are young, but they will deal with this simple equation all of their lives. Here are a few lessons on using choices and consequences in your discipline strategy.

Involve your child in consequential decision-making. If you ask your children, "If you choose to disobey me and turn on the TV when you know you are not allowed to have it on, what would be a good consequence for your behavior?" don't expect your children to say, "Actually, Mom, I understand exactly what you are saying. If I turn on the TV, you will have the right to take the TV away from me for an entire weekend. If I do it a second time, then I'm grounded from the TV for a week. A third time really needs to have a major consequence, like no soccer for two weeks. And, Mom, thanks for looking out for me and my future. I will be a much more responsible adult and marriage partner because of these TV consequences." *Right!* When it comes to creating consequences, don't expect your children to have much of a positive response; however, when the consequences to various actions have been discussed ahead of time and your children have helped decide the consequences, they will tend to accept more of the results of their choices.

Just this week, Rebecca, our fourteen-year-old, went to the park five houses away from our home without telling us. Obviously, this is not an offense worth capital punishment. However, she knew the Burnses' rules on going someplace without telling us. The only way we knew she was at the park was that her older sister had seen her talking with some of her friends as she drove past the park. As much as I didn't want to embarrass Rebecca, a deal is a deal and a consequence is a consequence. I drove to pick her up. She balked a little but got in the car. The first words out of her mouth were, "I'm busted! I should have asked you or Mom."

"You're right, Rebecca," I answered. "The crazy thing is I would have been glad to allow you to go to the park or invite your friends to our house."

She asked, "What's my consequence?"

"You tell me, Rebecca."

"No phone or computer for the day?"

"Right!"

"Can I go back to the park, Dad?"

"No, you lost that privilege for the day."

I wish I could tell you it always goes that smoothly. At home we never know what any of our reactions will be. Since Rebecca had been a part of discussing and creating the consequences in the first place, she could be frustrated with me, but she also knew she had already signed off on the consequence for not telling us where she was going. She also knows that the consequences get stiffer if she does it again, and by the third time she loses the privilege of a very special school experience that she is looking forward to participating in. Remember, your job is not to try to be your children's best friend, but rather to train them to be responsible adults.

Consequences must match the problem. Our children should expect minor consequences for minor infractions and major consequences for major infractions. Some parents tend to panic when their children begin to rebel just a bit. We must be consistent and not overreact to children moving toward independence. If they are a few minutes late on curfew or didn't clean up their rooms, it doesn't mean just because you had a bad day that they need to be placed on restriction for the rest of their lives.

When we pass out consequences that don't match the problem, we usually renege on the consequence anyway, and that produces inconsistent discipline and more potential problems. At the same time, if your child is continuing to be disobedient over a period of time and you don't offer a consequence that matches the problem, you are not teaching him or her the lifelong lesson your child needs or deserves. As Proverbs 26:27 reminds us, "If a man digs a pit, he will fall into it; if a man rolls a stone, it will roll back on him."

Discipline calmly. We can't find any Italian blood in our family trees (although we sure like pizza!), but our house is anything but tranquil most of the time. Here's our goal: We don't give out discipline when we are angry; otherwise, we'll usually say or do something we don't mean.

Leave the phrase "you will never" out of your discipline vocabulary. Don't tell your kids that they are out of the school play unless you really, really mean it. Threats don't work! When we are angry or full of empty threats, we are often not very consistent with our consequences and discipline. Sending mixed messages to our kids usually gets in the way of the lesson we are trying to teach them.

Express your expectations clearly. In other words, the consequences must make sense to your child. If we constantly offer unrealistic expectations, then we are most likely not doing an effective job in the discipline department. Be absolutely clear, ask your children to tell you what they understand, and if you must, write down your expectations.

Saturday morning is workday around the Burns house. For most of our seventeen years of child rearing, parenting has been more of a hassle than a joy. We finally decided to take on a different approach that seems to be working for the moment. We write down on a paper each of the agreed-upon chores for Saturday morning. If our kids want to do anything from watching TV to spending time with their friends, they know that all requests happen after the chores are finished. Should they choose not to do chores, then they are making the decision not to spend time doing fun weekend activities. If they want to sit in their pajamas all day and delay their chores, that's up to them—as long as it doesn't get in the way of other family activities. "Freedom comes after chores" is our motto. Right now, it's working, but for us it must be on paper, and we must let the kids know we mean business when it comes to consequences.

THE FAMILY CONTRACT

Perhaps one of the most effective consequence and discipline tools is what many call the "family contract." Basically the family contract involves discussing and then putting on paper the expectations and agreements about certain behaviors or issues in the family. The family contract helps kids discipline themselves. You will find that the clearer you are with the issue and consequence, the easier it is to manage a family contract. Don't go overboard and make their entire lives a family contract, or you will lose the powerful results of the contract. Focus on behaviors, and their attitudes will follow. Keep your contract simple, and whenever possible, have your children help create the family contract because people support what they create.

Here are a couple of examples of family contracts:

Simple Family Contract

Issue: Sloppy habits at the dinner table

Expectation: Good table manners

Positive Consequences
- A general feeling of happiness and contentment
- After a week of good table manners, a special treat or dessert
- After a month, an art project or special weekend outing to celebrate the victory

Negative Consequences
- No TV for the evening
- Go to bed a half-hour early
- Remove phone privilege

A More Severe Family Contract

Issue: A failing grade. You have already tried other methods to bring up the grade.

Expectations: Raising the grade to a C with zero tolerance for not turning in homework

Action steps
- Weekly progress report signed from teachers
- Daily homework assignments signed by teachers

- Daily homework check-in with Mom after school and Dad at the end of the evening

- Weekly check-in time with Dad about school, grades, and attitude

- Consequence: You may choose to be in the school play. If you do not choose to do the agreed-upon schoolwork, then you are choosing to take yourself out of the play. (This is called reality discipline.)

Positive Consequences
- Teachers will not have to sign the daily homework sheets

- After a C grade, we will not need to have a weekly progress report

- If the grade is an A or B, then we celebrate with a new outfit or special event

Negative Consequences
- We have a meeting with the school counselors and teachers

- We remove phone or weekend privileges

- If nothing else works, then we consider homeschooling or changing schools

I know one dad whose son was caught ditching class. After the second time, the dad sat in class with his son for two weeks. His son never ditched again! This is a bit harsh for some families, but clear and expressed expectations of behavior are a must. A family can use contracts or understandings such as those listed here, but regardless of the method, children do better when they have a crystal-clear understanding of what is expected and the consequences of not following through on the understanding. Below are two other tools some families use to help their kids and themselves work on constancy.

FAMILY RULES

The Rules as I Understand Them	The Reason for the Rules	Negative Consequences	Positive Consequences
1.			
2.			
3.			
4.			
5.			

Here's a simple family rules sheet:

ULTIMATE DISCIPLINE CHECKLIST

1. The behavior I want changed is _____.

2. How might I be feeding or enabling the problem behavior?

3. Will I give the child a choice or is the behavior a must?

4. My clearly stated rule is_____.

5. The consequences are_____.

6. My follow-through will be_____.

7. Will I be consistent no matter what it takes?

KEEP YOUR CHILD'S SPIRIT OPEN

The simple phrase "rules without relationship leads to rebellion" is so very true when it comes to keeping a child's spirit open in the midst of discipline. A friend of mine with many problems as an adult once told me, "I was scared to death of my dad. He ruled with his fist and the belt. He forced obedience in the house when he was there, but every one of us moved out as quickly as we could and had problems dealing with intimacy and relationships partly because of the way Dad handled us as children." When it comes to discipline, your kids need you to always show respect even in the midst of tension. You can disagree with your child and still be able to communicate.

Nagging sure isn't the best way to keep your child's spirit open. Sometimes we simply need to have the self-control to keep our mouths shut for the time being and find a better and more effective way to share our concerns with our children or spouse. I've never heard a kid tell me that he or she greatly benefited from Mom or Dad's nagging. Nagging is a lazy habit many of us get involved with or even imitate from our own parents. However, there is a better way to discipline and a better way to communicate.

Choose your battles wisely. The parent who tends to become defensive is the parent who is trying to manage too many battles on too many fronts. Does your child's room need to be as perfect as your room? If that is your battle, then win the fight; but if it isn't the issue to fight for, then compromise.

Cathy is much more of a "neatnic" than any of the rest of us. When we were first married, we had to find a satisfactory settlement on clean rooms. Over the years Cathy has trained me to pick up my clothes, to put the dishes away, and not to leave stuff everywhere. Unfortunately, she now has three daughters who, thank God, look more like their mom but clean more like their dad. The compromise isn't always easy for Cathy. We've negotiated that we expect clean rooms on Tuesdays and Saturdays. That's two more days than our girls would choose and five fewer days than Cathy would like. But we've chosen compromise and negotiation, since it's just not the battle to close each other's spirits over.

Communication is key to keeping the spirit open. Many parents need some improvement in the areas of eye contact, tone of voice, and body language. Often our body language tells our children more than our words about our availability. Listening is the language of love, and empathy will be more valuable than you will ever imagine in keeping the spirit from closing when you must discipline. Our kids have feelings, and we have to show respect for their feelings along with their privacy. Discern which areas of their lives are not critical for you to intervene in and then stay out of their business in those areas.

Your words can have power. Your words can either build up or destroy your children. When a child's spirit is broken and closing, it is often because they feel attacked by their parents' anger. You can attack the behavior, but not the person.

One family I talked to was having some major problems between the mom and the teenage daughter. This can be somewhat normal, but this daughter's spirit was almost totally closed to her mother. The young girl was definitely a spitfire. She might be called the poster child of the strong-willed child. I could see why there could be conflict, but I couldn't understand why the daughter's spirit was so closed to what seemed to be a very nice mom. Then the daughter gave me some insight. She told me when her mother got angry with her there were two constant themes. Her mother would lose control and say, "I hate you" or "You are the reason that your father and I got a divorce." Even if in her heart of hearts her mother had moments of believing those abusive words, she should have kept them to herself. The teenager felt rejected, hated, blamed, and attacked. Most of the time the mother was a good mom with a loving attitude. However, those powerful, destructive words were keeping the spirit of her daughter closed toward her. Anger isn't what gets kids to obey. Action, love, and consistency are what work.

Disciplining with consistency is one of the answers to having a happy, healthy family. What's amazing about discipline is that it takes an incredible amount of parental discipline to be consistent and to clearly express your expectations. Just about the time we resolve to make the right discipline decisions, our child manipulates us into moving away from our resolve. However, when you fail—and you will—pick yourself up and keep being consistent. Your kids will thank you twenty years from now. You may even have to do what one father did.

A father was pushing a stroller through a city park. The baby was screaming at the top of his lungs. It was a summer day, and the park was filled with people watching. As the embarrassed young father passed by, he was heard saying in a forced calm voice, "Take it easy, Malcolm. Now, now, just relax. No reason to get excited. Just calm down and everything will be all right. Come on, Malcolm, just settle down and trust the Lord." An older woman who was watching stopped the man and said, "My, what a nice baby. Did you say his name was Malcolm?" To which the frustrated father replied, "No, ma'am. His name is Joshua. I'm Malcolm." This young dad is to be admired for his determination not to lose his temper.

FURTHER READING

- Dobson, James. *The New Dare to Discipline*. Wheaton, Ill.: Tyndale, 1996.

- Leman, Ken. *Making Children Mind without Losing Yours.* Grand Rapids: Fleming H. Revell, 2000.

- Nelson, Jane. *Positive Discipline.* New York: Ballantine, 1996.

DISCUSSION STARTERS

1. How would you describe the type of discipline you received growing up?

2. In what way is your discipline similar to your parents' and in what way is it different?

3. Have you ever used a contract for your child? Did it work?

4. What elements in your life make it difficult, at times, to keep your child's spirit open?

5. How do the following proverbs relate to disciplining with consistency?

Train a child in the way he should go, and when he is old he will not turn from it. (Prov. 22:6)

If a man digs a pit, he will fall into it; if a man rolls a stone, it will roll back on him. (Prov. 26:27)

5

RUTHLESSLY
ELIMINATE STRESS

I feel absolutely dry and overextended. I'm a people pleaser by nature, and I feel like my busyness is letting others down. My overload is affecting my intimacy with Cathy, and I don't feel as close to my daughters right now. I'm busy being with people, but I'm feeling lonely. Many a day I do not look forward to work because I know that I will have to deal with the urgent and not the most important. I'm tired and fatigued. I want to work out and eat better, but I keep putting off what is healthy for what is easy. I'm craving friendships, and I'm too busy to even attempt to get together with some of the guys. God is getting some of my attention, but not what I dreamed it would be by this time in my life. I used to be a lot more fun.

—Taken from my journal

PERHAPS THE GREATEST PROBLEM in parenting is the breathless pace at which we live our lives. I love the story of the first grader who wondered why her father brought home a briefcase full of work every evening. Her mother explained, "Daddy has so much to do that he can't finish it all at the office." "Well then," asked the child innocently, "why don't they put him in a slower group?" As the pace of life gets more and more unhealthy perhaps it is time to join the "slower group."

There are no easy answers in this chapter, just difficult decisions. Are you experiencing what some like to call the overload syndrome? It's what Richard Swenson calls "margin."[1] Margin is the space that once existed between our load and our limits. Margin is the space between vitality and exhaustion. It is our breathing room, our reserves, our leeway. Unfortunately, few families have much room for margin in our over-committed, crisis-mode lives. As a friend of mine says, "We work hard, we play hard, and we crash hard."

You probably already know if the overload syndrome is plaguing your life and your family, but just in case, answer these questions:

1. Have you stopped enjoying life because you are too busy?
2. Have you stopped developing new relationships?
3. Are you exhausted most of the time?
4. Do you and your spouse have a regular date night?
5. Does your family have an enjoyable dinner together on a regular basis?
6. Do you get enough hours of sleep?
7. Do you take a restful day off?
8. Do you have regular proactive family times together?
9. Do you have credit problems or a large debt load?
10. Are your children showing signs of stress?

If you struggle with many of these questions, then you are among the majority of families who are living in crisis mode. Let me be blunt: You are flirting with disaster. That disaster is either yours, your spouse's, or your children's. Crisis-mode living paralyzes families.

Crisis-mode living is when you spend every waking moment of almost every day trying to figure out how to keep all your plates spinning in the air. In crisis mode you keep running faster and faster, from project to project, deadline to deadline, quota to quota, meeting to meeting, folding laundry to carpool to . . . you get the picture. Your life's rpm is in the red, and you believe you have no other option but to keep on running, faster and faster. If you stop, you fear the plates will crash. And frankly, some of the plates will crash if you stop; but if you don't stop soon, the results may be much worse on the physical, emotional, and spiritual health of you and your family. Healthy families have figured out how to live with balance and margin.

Here's what happens when we live in crisis mode for too long. We begin to skim relationally. If you are married, your bond with your spouse that was once strong and intimate becomes weak and distant. Virtually all our relationships are damaged by hurry. Many families are relationally starved because of overcommitment and fatigue. Frankly, sometimes our children lie wounded, run over by high-speed intentions. Our children have watched more videos than is healthy simply because we don't have the strength. When we skim relationally, friendships slip away. We quit our support groups and miss our family outings. We find our relationships fading. Friendships that were deep and meaningful are now characterized as shallow. Casual relationships hardly even exist. Pretty soon no one has access to our souls.

Crisis mode even causes us to skim spiritually. What was once a burning desire to serve God has become relegated to a few prayers and a dull faith—the kind of faith we said that we would never have. In Eugene Peterson's beautiful translation of the Bible, he paraphrases the apostle Paul talking about people like you and me. "They were so absorbed in their 'God projects' that they didn't notice God right in front of them, like a huge rock in the middle of the road. And so they stumbled into him and went sprawling" (Romans 9:32 MSG).

Crisis-mode living also causes us to skim emotionally. When we are too busy we tend to ignore the emotional side of our lives. You may find your anger flares up more than it used to, and you don't take the time to figure out why. Our patience with our children wears thin. When we are in crisis mode, we quit paying attention to feelings like hurt, sadness, or guilt. We become mechanical soldiers marching through our days just maintaining, doing what's necessary, and stuffing our feelings deeper and deeper inside our lives. We are emotionally depleted, but we keep on pushing. The results aren't pretty!

It was the great philosopher Vince Lombardi of the Green Bay Packers who told his teams over and over again, "Fatigue makes cowards of us all." I know I am a lousy husband to Cathy, a poor excuse for a father to my children, and a mediocre president of YouthBuilders when I'm fatigued and living in crisis mode. I have a sign in my office that simply reads, "If the devil can't make you bad, he'll make you busy." Most families are so busy doing good things that they miss doing what is most important.

I love to sit in our family's spa. When we turn up the heat and turn on the jets, my burdens seem to disappear. My most relaxing spot in life is right in the backyard sitting in that spa, feeling the pressure of the jets on my back and the pressures in my life fade away for the moment. One night we were going to have a family meeting in the spa. My daughters know I'm a pushover when I'm sitting in the spa.

Why it takes us men so much less time to change clothes and put on a swimsuit to jump in the spa I have no idea. But on this night, as most times, I was in the spa a good ten minutes before my three daughters and my wife. Actually, I didn't mind much because those jets felt so good against my back and my pressures were fading away, when the jets stopped. As I now soaked in the hot water, I noticed for the first time that our spa was filthy. We had experienced a windstorm, and the spa had collected leaves, dirt, and just plain old grime. I had been sitting in filth, but because of the jets churning up all the dirt, I hadn't even noticed.

As I heard the girls and Cathy coming, I realized I had two options: I could either take the time to get out of the spa and clean all the grease and grime, or I could quickly turn the jets back on and my family would never realize they were sitting in dirty water. So what do you think I did? Need I ask? I quickly turned back on those jets, and we had our family meeting in our polluted spa. They never knew!

Unfortunately too many of us live our lives like that. We seldom take the time to deal with our life issues and problems; instead, we just keep on pushing, hoping that the marriage will get better or that the subtle negative signs we are seeing from our kids will disappear by osmosis. Well, they don't. A happy, healthy family builds margin into their lives and deals with the problems and issues in front of them before they become catastrophes. For too many years, I have heard myself say to Cathy, "As soon as we get past this season in our lives, then it will slow down." But seasons turn into years, the crisis mode often continues, causing more reasons to skim relationally, emotionally, and spiritually.

HEALTHY HOMES HAVE LESS STRESS
AND MORE MARGIN

How does a family overcome the disease of the overload syndrome? No easy answers here, just some important but sometimes difficult decisions.

Healthy families are made, not born. So let's roll up our sleeves and get to work. The sacrifice is real, but the payoff is well worth it.

The unbalanced life will not be kind to the areas we neglect. One of the most famous business writers of this century recently wrote, "A successful business person usually has to give up a great deal to succeed. Few people I know can be a success in their business life and take the time to coach their son's Little League team." When I first read his statement, I was angry. Who does he think he is giving some dads who are already doing a poor job as fathers the idea that to be successful you have to sacrifice even more time with your children? Why can't you be successful at both parenting and business? Believe me I know several men and women who are successful at both.

However, I think the business author is actually right. The successful businessperson almost always sacrifices family time to make it to the top. So as a person who wants to be successful in my career *and* have healthy family relationships, I've had to learn, sometimes the hard way, this principle: "The unbalanced life will not be kind to the areas we neglect." Go ahead. Coach your son's Little League team and take a few more years to climb the corporate ladder. But for goodness' sake, don't neglect your family.

Since I believe in the power of being there for my kids, I spend less time in the office, which means fewer things get done. It means turning down speaking engagements that would help my career. It means rearranging a flight to be at my daughter's homecoming game and flying the red-eye to speak the next day, tired. In order to practice the power of being there with your kids and live a more balanced life, you must give up some of your other interests. Yes, you will probably lose some profit in the short run; but if you neglect your family and your marriage for the sake of the business, you will reap the results of an unbalanced family life. If you focus on your family as a priority, then you often simply won't be as successful in your business. See I told you it wouldn't always be easy! But if your schedule is constantly out of control, then your long-term effectiveness as a parent is at risk.

I would nominate Tom Yankoff for "Dad of the Year." Successful in business, you bet. A terrific and involved dad, no doubt. But Tom wasn't always a nominee for Dad of the Year. He was the typical competitive businessman who showed his love for his family by working hard and long hours. The money started coming in, and the square footage in his new house improved dramatically. He drove nice cars, his family took nice vacations, and his kids attended the prestigious private school in his area. They looked like the all-American, rich, successful, healthy, and churchgoing family.

Tom was too busy to think much about the occasional gnawing feeling that all was not right at home. He knew that his marriage to Dina was stale, but he really did not want to work on it. She was encouraging him to attend counseling with her, but that only ticked him off. After all, they weren't crazy. Sure, his anger flared and, yes, he wasn't always there for his two sons even when he was present. After all, he had a lot to do and a lot on his mind. His two boys were making him a bit nervous. They were straying a bit from their morals and values, but Tom figured that boys would be boys. Many times he came home to conflict that he was often too tired to deal with, so he either settled the problem with his anger or hid behind more work or sleep or sometimes even church involvement. Maybe a good vacation would solve their family problems.

Tom wasn't a bad guy. He went to church. He voted! He skimmed relationally with his family, but in his mind he figured, *What successful person doesn't?* He and his wife came from classic dysfunctional families. So what is normal anyway? He actually was proud of himself that he had taken the time to plan a very special family ski trip. He would reconnect and have a great time with his boys and Dina. His office could surely function without him for four days! On the first day of skiing, he and his older son, Trevor, jumped on the ski lift to go straight to the top of the mountain. He looked over at Trevor, and it was as if he was hit in the head. He stared at his son, whom he deeply loved, and he realized that he didn't know the names of his son's friends or if he liked a special girl. He couldn't name any of his teachers. He didn't know his son's favorite color. The more Tom thought about what he didn't know about his son, the worse it became in his mind. By the time they slid off the chair lift, Tom was in tears. Trevor had no idea what was going on. Was his dad having a heart attack or a nervous breakdown? After three hours of talking and praying and crying—the emotional release of his life—Tom skied down the hill and quit his job!

Pretty dramatic decision, huh? Tom knew he needed more than just correcting a few out-of-balance habits. He had to give up his mistress, which was his job. Tom signed on as the boys' football booster club president. He went to counseling with Dina for their marriage. He joined a men's support and accountability group at his church. He found time to reconnect with his family. Of course he had to find another job, but this time he came into it with his eyes open and with God's help decided that he would build a support system to keep his family priorities in balance.

Today, Tom has led the way for his family to be part of the transitional generation of people who will live a healthier life than the previous generation. Plus, both of his children would definitely nominate him as Dad of the Year. Have you ever met a person who said, "I wish my mom or dad would have spent more time at the office when I was growing up?" I haven't.

If the devil can't make you bad, he'll make you busy. I like the story of the man whose life was notoriously cluttered, busy, and confused. After he died, the epitaph etched on his tombstone read, "Organized at last." When it comes to adding more activities to our already overcrowded lifestyles, there is a word in the English language that far too many families don't use enough—the word *no!* Should we add one more event to our already crowded schedule? No! Lindsey is in soccer, church youth group, drama club, and tennis, but could she still squeeze in piano? No, she can't. Even if she wants to add another activity, is it really worth it? Far too many kids are growing up with too much stress because they are just too busy doing good things. Two words of advice for the busy schedule are *eliminate* and *concentrate*. As crazy as this may seem, I want to give you permission to cut back and do less. More is not always better. Doesn't it feel good when you finally get around to cleaning out the closet? Do you really miss the stuff you threw away? I doubt it. If you slow your pace down a bit, you'll feel better and so will your family. Cathy has a favorite saying to me that hits me right where it counts, in my heart. "Jim, we already have a Messiah who has done wonderfully for more than two thousand years. Don't replace him!"

Cutting back involves resting and relaxing. Rest must be a non-negotiable time in your schedule and in your family's schedule. Rest heals, soothes, and gives perspective. For the generation who invented the 24/7/365 mentality, it is important to remember that even God rested on the seventh day of creation. "In six days the LORD made the heavens and the earth, and on the seventh day He rested and *was refreshed*" (Exod. 31:17 NKJV; emphasis added). Refreshment is such a great concept.

When Cathy and I celebrated our twenty-fifth wedding anniversary, we took a ten-day "do nothing and plan nothing" trip up to the beautiful British Columbia coastline in Canada. The tranquil setting, the long walks, the lingering over meals, the loving, tender touch was exactly what we needed to clean up some of the cobwebs of our relationship and return to our deep love of twenty-five years prior. We rested and were replenished. We came home wondering why we waited so long to have those kinds of experiences.

When was the last time you were refreshed? When was the last time you proactively replenished your family relationship? It was probably longer ago than you wish, and you are most likely looking for the next time as soon as possible. Sometimes people will stop me and say, "You must be really busy." Yes, I am busy, but they mean to equate busyness with success. How unfortunate that some of the busiest people we know are some of the unhappiest people who rarely take time to rest and relax.

Here's a fairly simple question. Do you take at least a twenty-four-hour day off from your work? This includes homemakers! Of course the kids still need to be fed, but do you ever rest? According to authorities, North Americans are busier than ever and rest less than any time in our history. If you are not taking at least a twenty-four-hour rest from your work, I believe you are pressing toward burnout, if you are not already there. Most likely if you do not have times of quality rest, then your primary relationships are in dishevel. Your primary relationships are with your spouse, children, special friends, God, and even how you treat yourself. Rest won't restore a broken marriage or put a poor relationship with your child magically back together, but it sure will get you started in the right direction.

Sometimes I work too hard and take life too seriously. Last week I noticed flowers in my backyard in full bloom, and I had missed the process of blooming. Life is too short. Sometimes we need to sit back and enjoy God's gift to us. It's time for another generation to be reminded of Brother Jeremiah's advice as he reflected on his many years of Christian service toward the end of his life:

If I had my life to live over again, I'd try to make more mistakes next time. I would relax. I would limber up. I would be sillier than I have been this trip. I know of very few things I would take seriously. I would take more trips. I would climb more mountains, swim more rivers, and watch more sunsets. I would do more walking and looking; I would eat more ice cream and fewer beans. I would have more actual troubles and fewer imaginary ones.

You see, I am one of those people who live prophylactically and sensibly and sanely, hour after hour, day after day. Oh, I've had my moments, and if I had it to do over again, I'd have more of them. In fact, I'd try to have nothing else. Just moments, one after another, instead of living so many years ahead each day. I have been one of those people who never go anywhere without a thermometer, a hot water bottle, a gargle, a raincoat, aspirin, and a parachute. If I had it to do over again, I would go places, do things, and travel lighter than I have.

If I had my life to live over, I would start barefooted earlier in the spring and stay that way later in the fall. I would play more. I would ride on more merry-go-rounds. I'd pick more daisies.[2]

FIGHT FOR SOLITUDE

Do you ever take time to be silent? I am by no means an expert on living life as a monk, but there is great health and peace found in solitude. As you read the New Testament, you will often see that the strength Jesus found to be with energy-draining people was found in his quiet moments. Often right before a very busy time of ministry he would go away to a lonely place and pray. (See Luke 6:12ff. and Mark 1:35ff.)

The spiritual discipline of solitude has been lost in our twenty-first-century hurried lifestyles. However, healthy families ruthlessly eliminate as much hurry and clutter from their lives as possible and pursue moments of solitude. Spiritually speaking, solitude is being with God and God alone. Is there space for solitude in your life? In solitude you will hear the whisper of God's voice saying, "You are my beloved, the apple of my eye. You are doing a wonderful job parenting those kids. I treasure you, I forgive you, and I believe in you. You are my child, and we are in this parenting thing together."

If you never find time for solitude, then you will hear another voice shouting at you, "You aren't good enough; you are a failure as a parent and spouse. You aren't spiritual enough or pretty enough or rich enough. Your life is a waste." But in solitude we hear the voice of God reassuring us that he loves us and is proud of us. If you keep that thought in mind and find moments of solitude and rest, then you can deal with an enormous amount of failure as well as an enormous amount of success because your identity is based on the unfailing love of God as opposed to family inconsistencies.

In solitude I ask myself three questions that help me find perspective:

1. Do I like the human being I am becoming?

2. Is the work of God I'm doing with vocation and family destroying the work of God in me?

3. How often does my family receive only my emotional scraps?

Many times I do not like the answers I give to these questions in the quiet moments of my soul. Busyness paralyzes our souls, but solitude and rest bring us hope.

CHILDREN AND STRESS

Adult stress-related diseases have never been worse, and authorities tell us that adult stress-related disease has its roots in childhood. It's a simple fact that stressed-out parents almost inevitably pass their stress along to their children. The only good stress is stress that is short-lived. The medical, psychological, and spiritual authorities agree that stress is affecting our children in negative ways. Our stressed-out children today are in poor shape physically, mentally, and spiritually. Parents must do something to ease stress in their children's lives.

The good news of this chapter is that once you understand where the stress in your home is coming from and how it affects your child, you are well on the road to preventing more stress damage in the life of your child. Gordon and Vicki were living the very busy life of a pastor and spouse in a very successful church. Their home was filled with love, but because of the family's extremely busy schedule, the children didn't have a regular bedtime. Both children kept getting sick and often missed school, which was affecting their grades and self-image.

Finally, Vicki had a long talk with the family pediatrician. This gentleman was active in their church and knew the lifestyle of this busy family. He sat Vicki down in his office and said, "I have a hunch why things are physically deteriorating with your children and why both of them are struggling with school. Vicki, you and Gordon are too busy and the kids do not have a regular enough schedule or specific bedtime routine. Your kids are great kids, but they are sleep-deprived."

Vicki didn't expect this answer; she and Gordon had considered getting the kids tested for ADD and other learning disorders. Gordon and Vicki took the doctor's advice, and both sacrificed their work schedules to give their children more of a routine and definitely more sleep. Within three months, both of their children had raised their grades from Ds to Bs, and the entire atmosphere of their home had dramatically improved.

Gordon and Vicki are my heroes because they recognized there was a problem, sought advice, and then made some readjustments to their lives to guard their children from more stress than they could handle. It takes courage and sacrifice to make bold decisions, but that is exactly what some families must do to stress-proof their home.

IS YOUR CHILD OVERSTRESSED?

Take the excellent "Is My Child Overstressed?" test. This test was created by one of the world's most outstanding authorities on stress, Dr. Archibald Hart. Hart is insightful when he says, "Today's children are faced with double jeopardy. They face a world that is more stressful than ever. In addition, they are forced to depend less and less on their traditional source of support—their families."[3]

STRESS TEST: IS MY CHILD OVERSTRESSED?[4]

Child's name_____

Carefully review your child's behavior and complaints for the previous two or three weeks and rate the following questions using this scale:

> 0 = My child infrequently feels or experiences this.
>
> 1 = My child sometimes (perhaps once a month) experiences this.
>
> 2 = My child experiences this often (between once a month and once a week).
>
> 3 = My child experiences this frequently (more than once a week).

1. My child complains of headaches, backaches, or general muscle pains or stiffness. _____

2. My child reports stomach pains, digestive problems, cramps, or diarrhea. _____

3. My child has cold hands or feet, sweaty palms, or increased perspiration. _____

4 My child has a shaky voice, trembles and shakes, displays nervous tics, or grinds and clenches his or her teeth. _____

5. My child gets sores in the mouth, skin rashes, or low-grade infections like the flu. _____

6. My child reports irregular heartbeats, skipped beats, thumping in the chest, or a racing heart. _____

7. My child is restless, unstable, and feels "blue" or low. _____

8. My child is angry and defiant and wants to break things. _____

9. My child has crying spells, and I have difficulty stopping them. _____

10. My child overeats, especially sweet things. _____

11. My child seems to have difficulty in concentrating on homework assignments. _____

12. My child reacts intensely (with angry shouting) whenever he or she is frustrated. _____

13. My child complains of a lot of pain in many places of the body. _____

14. My child seems anxious, fidgety, and restless, and he or she tends to worry a lot. _____

15. My child has little energy and has difficulty getting started on a project. _____

Total: _____

Test Interpretation

0–5   Your child is remarkably low in stress or handles stressful situations extremely well.

6–12   Your child is showing minor signs of stress. While it is nothing to be concerned about, some attention to stress control may be warranted.

13–20   Your child is beginning to show signs of moderate stress. Some attention should be given to how your child copes with stress.

21–30   Your child is showing significant signs of stress. You should give urgent attention to helping him or her reduce stress levels.

Over 30 Your child appears to be experiencing very high stress levels. You should do everything possible to eliminate stressful situations until your child can learn to cope. You may want to consider getting professional help.

Note: You may want to go over the test items that have been answered with a rating of 2 or above to better understand the signs of stress in your child's life. See where you can provide relief and help your child build more resistance to stress. If you feel that your child's problems, no matter what his or her score on this test, are beyond your ability to handle, then seek immediate professional help.

After you have taken the test, you will want to make sure that you remember the possible symptoms of stress in your child. There are physical symptoms and emotional symptoms of stress. Sometimes it is difficult to discern what is normal child or adolescent behavior and what has its roots in stress-related disease. If you see those symptoms in your own children or are confused about them, then I would strongly suggest that you seek the help of a counselor or pastor. The Bible is clear, "Where there is no counsel, the people fall; but in the multitude of counselors there is safety" (Prov. 11:14 NKJV).

The key physical symptoms to look for are headaches, dizziness or lightheadedness, heartburn, stomach problems, generalized body pain, grinding of teeth, skin eruptions, frequent infections or minor illnesses, sleeplessness, and loss of appetite, to name a few. The emotional symptoms are sometimes more difficult to determine, but they include anxiety and panic reactions, depression, general lethargy, outbursts of anger, and irritability.

STRESS-PROOF YOUR KIDS

If you see stress as a problem in your home, then it is time to reexamine your lifestyle in order to help your children succeed. First, start with the basics like getting adequate sleep, keeping physically fit, providing plenty of room in your schedule for relaxing, and making sure that you don't overcommit. If you try these basic but not necessarily easy steps and things are still not improving, then it is time to get a professional involved before more problems arise, since so much of the stress-related disease we see in adults has its roots in childhood.

FURTHER READING

Richard Swenson is one of my favorite authors on the subject of stress. Here are two great books I'd recommend.

- Swenson, Richard A. *Margin: Restoring Emotional, Physical, Financial, and Time Reserves to Overloaded Lives.* Colorado Springs: NavPress, 1995.

- Swenson, Richard A. *The Overload Syndrome: Learning to Live within Your Limits.* Colorado Springs: NavPress, 1999.

DISCUSSION STARTERS

1. How would you characterize the stress you have?
   - Extremely overcommitted and fatigued. In need of margin.
   - Managing our stress fairly well.
   - Not a problem in our home.

2. "The unbalanced life will not be kind to the areas we neglect." What concerns do you have with your family in this area right now?

3. What difficult decision might you have to make to ruthlessly eliminate stress for you and your family?

4. If you took the child's stress test, how did your children fare?

5. How does the following scripture challenge or give hope to you and your family?

Even youths grow tired and weary, and young men stumble and fall; but those who hope in the LORD will renew their strength. They will soar on wings like eagles; they will run and not grow weary, they will walk and not be faint. (Isa. 40:30–31)

6

COMMUNICATION IS
THE KEY

My boyhood goal had always been to play on the La Palma Little League All-Star team. It was now a reality. We were playing West Anaheim and I was pitching. What should have been a dream come true became a nightmare.

It started in the first inning: The lead-off hitter walked, the second guy hit a shot to right center field for a double, then I walked the third batter. With the bases loaded, I hung a curve ball and the clean-up hitter cleaned up! He put that curve ball over the fence for a grand slam. Ouch!

I felt humiliated.

After only four batters, the coach moved me to shortstop, where I made three errors in the next five innings! I also struck out twice. Needless to say, it wasn't a good day.

But now it was the last inning, and I had a chance to redeem myself. We were tied up, 6–6, and the bases were loaded as I walked up to bat. Until this day, I had the best batting average in the league. Despite my earlier strikeouts, everyone seemed confident that I could win the game for La Palma.

First pitch—I watched it go right over the plate: strike one. Second pitch caught the corner: strike two. I was feeling the tension. I stepped out of the batter's box and looked at my dad. He gave me the thumbs-up sign. The third pitch came straight down the middle of the plate. I watched it go by: strike three.

I almost single-handedly lost the game! The other team emerged as the champions.

I had never been more miserable in my life. I cried like a baby. I didn't want to talk to anyone, especially my dad. All my life he'd played catch with me, hit me grounders, and threw batting practice for me. He had always been there to instruct and encourage me. Now I'd let him down. I knew he'd be disappointed. I couldn't face him.

After unenthusiastically congratulating the other team, our coach told us it had been a great year. He said we should be proud. Yeah, right!

I couldn't put it off any longer. I had to face my dad. I slowly gathered my glove, bat, and jacket then looked up. There he was, running toward me. I knew I'd failed him. I was sure he was going to say something like, "You should never watch three strikes go by when the bases are loaded."

Instead he rushed over to me, gave me a big bear hug, and literally picked me up. Instead of anger, he had tears in his eyes. And he said, "Jimmy, I'm so proud of you."

That night we ate a couple of cheeseburgers and drowned our sorrows in chocolate milk shakes. He told me a story about a time he'd failed miserably in the most important game of the season. We laughed and cried together. My dad never was very mushy, but when I saw the tears in his eyes, I knew he loved me and that everything would be OK.

THAT DAY MY DAD COMMUNICATED unconditional love and acceptance to me. Recently, my eighty-two-year-old father came over to our house. We were sitting outside enjoying the warm California sunshine when I asked, "Dad, do you remember the Little League all-star game when I was twelve years old?"

"Oh sure, you struck out looking at the last pitch!" He smiled.

At forty-six years old, tears welled up in my eyes. "Dad, thanks for being so understanding back then. Even after I struck out you told me you loved me and that you were proud of me."

Now tears welled up in his eyes. "I am still proud of you."

"Thanks, Dad," I said, giving him a hug.

Later Cathy asked me, "What were you two talking about out there? It looked like you were crying."

"Oh, we were just remembering a Little League all-star game when I struck out with the bases loaded," I told her. I think Cathy's reply was something like, "Men are so strange!" That may be true, but he still communicated love to me.

When it comes down to it, the healthier the family, the more effective the communication. One of the primary problems of any dysfunctional family is lack of quality communication. Communication is behavior. It's an action word. It never stops. Communication is the means and not always only the goal. Communication is more about the interaction than the outcome. You can win the battle and lose the war in communication all the time.

When communication fails in a family, it is usually not because of the content, but rather the relationship. I always smile when I ask couples in premarital counseling, "How well do you communicate?" No one has ever said, "Horribly!" They usually respond to me by saying that they can tell each other "everything" or that they can talk for hours. One year after they are married I always invite them back for a conversation. Invariably, the couples say, "Our number one problem is communication."

A study was conducted at Michigan State University on communication between teenagers and parents. Dr. Gordon Sabine measured the responses of three thousand teenagers and their parents. The bottom line was that 79 percent of the parents interviewed thought they were communicating with their teenagers, but 81 percent of the teenagers said that their parents were not communicating with them. Communication is about perception.

Most of us didn't grow up with very good role models for communication, and if we don't learn helpful tools, we will pass on poor communication skills to our children. No one would disagree that healthy communication takes focus, discipline, and hard work. Communication involves at least two aspects: content and relationship. The previous generation may be guilty of focusing more on the content of communication than relationship. However, when communication fails, as I mentioned, it is usually not because of the content, but generally the problem falls more in the area of relationship.

Do you remember the father in one of the most famous musicals ever made into a movie, *The Sound of Music?* Captain Von Trapp loves his children, but when he arrives home from his busy travels, he runs the house like the military. He gets his children's obedience, but Maria, the nanny who later becomes his wife, passionately begs for him to place relationship over content. Von Trapp's communication style was "captain to private." He had control for the moment. In the movie, his relationship with his children changed and evolved into a loving parent, and it made all the difference in the world.

Parents like Von Trapp who practice the "captain to private" type of communication are employing shame-based parenting. As we have discussed previously, shame-based parenting brings rules without relationship, which equals rebellion. In healthy communication between parent and child, there is positive give-and-take. The child knows who is boss, but the relationship is based on affection, warmth, and encouragement.

What's difficult about communication is that if our parents used shame-based parenting, we will lean in the same direction. If our parents tried the "high-volume solution," we will find ourselves doing the same when we are desperate. If sarcasm was a part of your family growing up, then odds are, you will need to work harder not to make this one of your communication killers with your spouse and children. There are several other communication killers, which include verbal overkill, classic put-downs, the argument shift, silent treatment, and the preacher. I actually think I have tried all of those at one time or another and discovered that they just don't work in the long run.

COMMUNICATION STRATEGIES THAT WORK

Listening is the language of love. One of the greatest gifts you can offer your children is the gift of listening. You show that they have great value to you when you listen. My problem is when my children are wrong or have a poor attitude, I want to immediately correct them instead of honor them by simply listening. A young girl recently said to me, "I've quit sharing and telling my mom anything because I know I will just get a lecture. Mom wants a relationship with me, but she is not willing to sometimes just listen to me and leave it at that." Good advice.

Active listening doesn't come easily for most parents. Yet truly taking the time to really pay attention, show empathy, and listen to our children may be the most important part of long-lasting and healthy communication between parent and child. Recently when discussing the need to listen more effectively, one mother said, "I try to listen. I really do. But I guess I rarely follow through. Too often I break into the middle of a story that I perceive isn't that important, or I already know where my child is going with it and give my opinion. Life is so complicated and busy that I wonder if my listening while multitasking ever bothers my children." Of course it does.

I think it is time to put down the newspaper or let the dishes wait or record the ball game and find ways to communicate by simply listening to our children talk. Effective listening qualities include a genuine desire to really listen to your child, a willingness to accept their feelings and emotions whether they are right or wrong, the ability to accept not always being right, a nonjudgmental attitude, eye contact, little fidgeting, showing appreciation to your child that you feel honored to have the kind of relationship in which they share their heart with you, and a willingness not only to listen, but to keep in touch and be supportive.

Five other love languages. I don't know Gary Chapman personally, but by the number of his books I have purchased to give away and times that I have suggested someone buy his marriage and parenting resources, I have probably helped purchase his family's home. His material on the five languages of love is a part of my life and communication vocabulary. Basically Chapman sums up excellent communication by saying we all have emotional and love tanks, and if we keep the tanks full, we will have good communication and relationship. If we gamble with our family and spouse by keeping those tanks near empty, communication is much more difficult. The five love languages Chapman identifies are

1. Words of affirmation

2. Quality time

3. Receiving gifts

4. Acts of service

5. Physical touch

Gary Chapman says that most of us have a primary love language and perhaps a strong secondary love language, although all of them can be important to good communication and relationship. Let's look at all five ways to express love and communication from Chapman's book *The Five Love Languages* and then try to figure out what primary love language will fill your children's tank as well as your spouse's. These words are adapted from the study guide in the back of his book.[1]

Words of affirmation. In training our children, we tend to criticize failure. If overdone, this can create devastating consequences in adult life. Determine to praise your child for every right thing during the next week. A minimum of two compliments a day is a good goal.

Quality time. Get down to your child's level. Discover his or her interests and learn as much about him or her as possible. Be totally present, giving your child undivided attention. Make time each day to give your child (or each of your children) at least a few minutes of quality time. Make it a priority.

Receiving gifts. Gifts, if overdone, can become meaningless and teach a child a false set of values. But periodic gifts, thoughtfully chosen and given with affirming statements such as, "I love you, so I got a special gift for you" can help meet a child's need for love. The next time you buy or make your child a gift, express your love verbally as you present the gift. (You may also express your love as you refuse to give your child something you think is inappropriate. "I love you, so I will not buy you a rattlesnake for a pet.")

Acts of service. Though you constantly perform acts of service for your children, the next time you complete a task especially meaningful to your child make sure that you say it means you love him or her. Pick a task that is not especially appealing to you, but very important to your child. Learn a new skill in the academic or mechanical area to become a more well-rounded parent.

Physical touch. Hugging, kissing, and appropriate touching are very important for the child's emotional tank. Consider the age, temperament, love language, etc., of each child and determine a unique approach in this area. As they get older you will need to be sensitive, but maintain a regular habit of touching for affirmation.

As you discover your child's primary love language, focus on speaking it regularly. But do not neglect the other four. The others will be even more meaningful once you are speaking your child's primary language.

Now ask yourself, Which of these communication love languages is my primary need? How about the primary needs of your spouse and children? Practice filling the "love tank" of each family member by communicating in his or her love language.

COMMUNICATE HONESTY AND INTEGRITY

You don't have to be perfect, but kids don't want to follow the leadership of a hypocrite either. The parent who tries to come across as perfect is making a big mistake. Believe it or not, apologies improve communication. Let your children know you are human. Admit your mistakes and take the perfection pressure off. Admitting your mistakes clears the channels for real communication and removes barriers that may be building up. Admitting mistakes promotes sharing and oftentimes creates warmth and understanding.

Admitting failures also limits unrestrained idealism. What I mean by this is if your children go too long observing unreal parents who act as if they have no problems or flaws, the eventual shock of watching parents fail can end up being destructive. When you are honest about your imperfections with your children, you open up the way for a more mature type of problem solving. If your kids feel valued enough that you would share a struggle or a hurt, they will most often respond as a mature person. One caution would be not to get in the habit of dumping all your problems or marriage issues on your children. They are your kids, not your counselors.

Several years ago, our family took a sabbatical from my work so I could finish writing my Ph.D. dissertation. We decided to pick up the family and move to Hawaii for three months. I know you feel sorry for us, but somebody had to do it! Cathy is an educator by training and I made it through high school, so we decided to homeschool our children during our time away. Things were going pretty well until I realized I could get a Ph.D. easier than help Christy with sixth-grade math. My definition of hell is a place where they do math word problems, and that is exactly what Christy was studying during our homeschooling experience in Hawaii.

One morning there was a great deal of tension in our home. The younger girls wanted to ditch school and go to the beach. They were grumpy. Cathy was reacting to their grumpiness while Christy and I were struggling through the worst math word problem in the universe. I was anxious to get to my dissertation, and Christy was anxious to get away from me. In the middle of the word problem, she snapped at me, and I went crazy. I'm embarrassed to admit it, but the veins in my neck exploded with anger. I verbally slayed Christy right there in our living room, with Cathy, Rebecca, and Heidi looking on in disbelief. Usually I'm the guy who is pretty even-keeled, but not this time. "How dare you,"

"Don't you understand," "How selfish can you get," and "Furthermore . . ."
Then I sent her to her room.

The house grew eerily quiet. My two younger girls had looks of fear, and Cathy's look was somewhere between disgust and disbelief that I would go crazy over a math word problem and a poor attitude. I decided it was time to get out of the house. I slammed the door for added effect and sat down at the water's edge. After about fifteen minutes of blaming everyone (including my own sixth-grade math teacher) but myself, I came to my senses and humbly walked back into the house. Cathy was back to working with the other girls, and Christy was still in her room. Cathy glanced up for a moment, saw my contrite expression, and pointed to Christy's room. I gave a gentle knock—no answer. I opened the door. She was lying on her bed with tears in her big green eyes. I came alongside her bed, got down to her level, and said, "Christy, I am so sorry. I hope you will forgive me. That was all about me and not about you." With tears in those big green eyes of hers, she put her arms out around me and said, "I forgive you, Daddy, and I'm sorry too."

A few years later, Christy was being "hormonal and emotional" with her mother. I was in the other room, but the whole house had stopped the engines of our work and chores to listen in on Christy and her mom having quite a disagreement. Christy was being rude, so I stepped in and very calmly told her to go to her room and cool down. I told her that I would be up in a few minutes and we would talk. She sputtered all the way up the stairs to her bedroom and slammed the door. It was just nice to have some peace and quiet as the rest of the family went back to homework, chores, and fixing dinner. Almost an hour later as dinner was about to be served, Cathy asked me how my talk with Christy had gone. Being the great father that I am, I had to admit to Cathy that I had enjoyed the peace so much that I had actually forgotten to go talk with her.

I hurried upstairs and tapped on her door. In a very quiet voice, she told me to come in. She was lying on her bed with tears in her big green eyes. She stood up, and before I could say a word, she blurted out, "Daddy, I am so sorry! That was all about me and not about you guys. Will you forgive me?"

"Of course I will, Christy. I love you and I'm proud of you. In fact, I think I've heard pretty much those same words before from someone else. Do you remember?"

"Of course I do, Daddy. And I love you and I'm proud of you too."

The moral of the story is be an authentic parent who isn't afraid to apologize when you see the need. Proverbs 10:9 says, "The man of integrity walks securely," and the children of the man or woman of integrity will walk securely also. The other moral of the story is don't do sixth-grade math word problems if it's not your specialty!

COMMUNICATION IS A TIME INVESTMENT

I disagree with the parenting specialists who say that if you can't give your kids a quantity of time, then give them quality time. I think your kids deserve both. I find that my finest discussions with my own children come during the quantity times, not the so-called quality times. I'll be driving one of the kids someplace and—bingo!—the conversation goes to a very important topic. I just slow the car down and get in as much time as possible. As we discussed in a previous chapter, proactive communication comes along when we spend a great deal of time with our children. It's easier to get that time when our children are younger, but it is never too late.

I find my best conversations happen around food. This week I connected with each of my girls over a quick meal or treat. This morning I took Rebecca for a bagel breakfast and then dropped her off at school. Then I turned around and took Christy to the same bagel shop before dropping her off—good conversations and a few more calories for me.

A friend of mine gives his kids a nightly backrub. He wanders into their rooms right about bedtime and begins massaging their backs. He tells me it is amazing how they begin to open up about their days when he starts rubbing their backs. Another friend writes her children letters. Usually a letter is better expressed and better remembered than verbal words. Many of us express ourselves far more effectively when we write than when we speak. Sure it takes time to find a card and write the note, but the dividend is that your communication lines stay wide open.

CONFLICT CAN BE A PATH TO DEEPER COMMUNICATION

"Dad, Heather just called. Can I go over to her house to watch a movie?"

"Rebecca, ask your mom." *In other words, I'm too distracted.*

"Mom, Dad said I should check in with you before I go over to Heather's house to watch a movie."

"Your dad said it was all right?"

Pause. "He didn't seem to mind."

"Have you finished your chores? Did your dad check your homework?"

No official answer.

"Dad said it was fine with him if it was OK with you. Heather could use some company because she had a really bad day." *Distraction from the question.*

"Well, all right, but be home by eight-thirty."

Twenty minutes later:

"Jim, why on earth did you let Rebecca go to Heather's house? She didn't even start her chores, her room is a mess, and it doesn't look like she finished her homework."

"Cathy, I didn't say she could go. I told her to check in with you."

"Jim, you could have asked about her chores, looked in her room, or even quit watching that game and either helped me with some of the work around here or at least checked on Rebecca's schoolwork."

Jim is now angry. After all he has spent a difficult day writing books on how to have healthy families. "Hey, Miss Perfect. Why didn't you check Rebecca's homework and chores, and if you didn't work so hard, maybe everybody around here would be a bit happier."

"You're just like your father!"

"Well, you're becoming just like your mom!"

Does that kind of conflict ever happen in your home? It sure does in mine. Conflict can either be a path to communication blockage and unloving behavior, or it can be a path to deeper communication, greater understanding, and loving behavior. When there is a conflict, the natural inclination for parents and their children is to get defensive and closed with an intent to protect. The defensive, closed path of conflict leads to avoiding personal responsibility for feelings, behavior, and consequences. When we take this negative pathway with conflict, we immediately move into shame-based parenting by trying to control through guilt, manipulation, and sometimes fear.

Another negative way of dealing with conflict is when we give up because we don't want conflict and give in to keep the peace at all costs. As children get older, some parents deal with conflict by becoming overly permissive and withdrawing emotionally from the situation. The result of taking the closed path for conflict—whether that is guilt, defensiveness, control, or being overly permissive—is that the children's self-images are eroded and they have feelings of tension, frustration, anxiety, and anger. If you stay defensive and closed with conflict, you will always wind up with more power struggles and burdens. In the short haul it may be easier to handle conflict by being defensive or closed in order to protect our own fragile self-images. However there is a better way.

Conflict can also be used with an intent to learn and go deeper toward intimacy. The better way to handle conflict is to try our best to be nondefensive and open to learn. With this in mind we must assume responsibility for our own feelings, behaviors, and consequences. Working through the conflict takes greater emotional involvement, but it is the loving way to care for yourself as well as your child.

Most of us didn't learn to handle conflict in a healthy manner, so this process of exploration makes us more vulnerable to being affected by our children's concerns. If you are in an open mode of conflict, you are willing to experience transitory pain or fear to get to the truth about the problem. It means being a bit less judgmental and exploring feelings like fears, protections, values, responsibility, pain, inadequacy, and our own vulnerability.

Recently, Christy and Rebecca were on an airplane with me. They were both wearing earphones and listening to CDs. This lack of communication is a pet peeve of mine. However, I had allowed them to bring the CD players on the plane. I tried to get their attention by snapping my fingers at them. Christy calmly said, "You're snapping your fingers at me like I'm a dog."

I "snapped" back, "If you weren't wearing those earphones, we could communicate."

She replied, "All you have to do is tell me, Dad. Plus, snapping is demeaning."

I wanted to get defensive. Instead I simply said, "You're right. I'll try to be more sensitive next time." Our conflict was resolved, and life moved on.

The positive side to being open versus closed in with conflict is your children will sense a greater feeling of security. They will be able to take on more personal responsibility and be less defensive in conflict because their self-image is intact. When you choose this path, I believe you will see an almost immediate increase in family unity, security, and peace in the home. Of course dealing with conflict does not mean that you as the parent do not have the last word or need to discipline your children with consistency. The Bible's instruction "He who spares the rod hates his son, but he who loves him is careful to discipline him" (Prov. 13:24) is the perfect illustration that as parents we are called to guide and lead our children toward a healthy lifestyle. Teaching them a healthy way to handle conflict is one of the most important ways we accomplish this. It will bring your family more and greater intimacy.

Whether it is in the area of conflict, listening skills, or just being too overcommitted to communicate, your children will follow your example in the world of family communication. This is an area of family relationships where the parents must take the lead. If we don't, our children will develop some of the same poor communication habits we may have inherited from our families. Now is the time to drop our defenses and put away the pride. Now is the time to develop intimacy in our family relationships by becoming more effective communicators. There is always room for improvement and, believe me, you set the pace for your children. If you find yourself needing help in the area of communication, there are excellent books, seminars, and counselors that can assist you. Don't delay. Communication is the key to a happy, healthy family.

FURTHER READING

These books are keys to your children's and spouse's hearts.

- Gary Chapman. *The Five Love Languages: How to Express Heartfelt Commitment to Your Mate.* Chicago: Northfield Publishing, 1992.

- Gary Chapman and Ross Campbell, M.D. *The Five Love Languages of Children.* Chicago: Northfield Publishing, 1997.

- Gary Chapman. *The Five Love Languages of Teenagers.* Chicago: Northfield Publishing, 2000.

DISCUSSION STARTERS

1. In which areas of communication and intimacy does your family struggle in their relationships?

2. Who in your life is a good role model for communicating and why?

3. Can you identify the love language of your spouse (if you are married) and each of your children?

4. How would you rate your family's ability to handle conflict and communicate during conflict?

1	3	5
Needs immediate attention	so-so	not perfect but do a good job

5. How can you use the advice of the following scripture in a practical way with your family?

Therefore encourage one another and build each other up, just as in fact you are doing. (1 Thess. 5:11)

Here's a questionnaire our family used to help us evaluate our family intimacy quotient as well as our level of communication.

RATE YOUR FAMILY IQ (INTIMACY QUOTIENT)

How close is your family? Dolores Curran, author of *Traits of a Healthy Family* (Ballantine, 1983), evaluates fifteen traits that go together to make healthy families. The following questions are adapted from her research.

How to Take This Test
Rate the intimacy quotient of your family by responding to the questions. Award yourself points for each answer as follows.

1 point:	We're definitely not there yet.
2 points:	This is sometimes true of our family.
3 points:	This is usually true of our family.

Then add up your total points. (There are two questions representing each trait—in random order.)

If your total score is

1–30	Your family has the potential to become an intimate family if you are willing to apply energy and determination to the process.
30–60	Your family has a strong foundation upon which to build further intimacy.
60–90	You are maintaining strong momentum in the direction of intimacy.

114

1. In our marriage, my spouse and I share power equally, complementing each other's strengths and weaknesses.

2. At the dinner table, our family shares more than food. We also share ideas, feelings, disappointments, and dreams.

3. If there is a conflict between a family tradition and an outside responsibility, the family tradition usually wins.

4. As parents, we allow our children freedom to make decisions in certain areas and expect them to accept the consequences of those decisions.

5. Our family shares together in at least one leisure activity a week.

6. As parents, we are aware of our children's facial expressions, body language, and physical gestures and from these pick up clues that lead us to ask appropriate questions and initiate honest discussion.

7. The basic, underlying mood of our family is hopeful and forward-looking; we have our sources of stress, but we consider them temporary and manageable.

8. When we are alone together, my spouse and I are vulnerable to each other and risk exposure of our deepest feelings.

9. We allow our children to make choices between various activities outside the family, but we do not allow these activities to interfere routinely with our leisure time together.

10. We have different rules for children of different ages.

11. We know what we believe, and we find strength in our faith.

12. We have a vision as a family and seek to be involved in something bigger than the quality of our relationships.

13. We have our share of problems, but we usually can see the positive in every situation, no matter how bad.

14. No matter how busy we are, our entire family eats a meal together at least once each day.

15. My spouse and I agree on what is right and wrong.

16. We make an effort to gather regularly with those in our extended family.

17. We refuse to remove obstacles from our children's lives that will potentially foster their growth and responsibility.

18. As parents, we occasionally spend time alone with each of our children.

19. We keep our work commitments under control and do not allow them to routinely crowd out family.

20. Although we go through rough periods, we stick together and try to make things right.

21. In our family, we make each other feel important by supporting each other in our failures as well as in our successes.

22. As parents, we allow our children to be exposed to situations in which they can gradually earn more trust or rebuild trustworthiness.

23. When conflicts arise, we give everyone a chance to speak and work at negotiating solutions before the conflicts become volatile.

24. Different personality styles and preferences are accepted within our family life.

25. Our definition of success is not based on promotions, possessions, or power, but in the quality of our service to others.

26. We laugh at ourselves and with each other, and we use humor to defuse potentially stressful situations.

27. As adults, we provide for our kids a value system out of which certain rules and accepted behaviors arise.

28. We present opportunities in our home for our children to prove their capabilities.

29. The underlying religious attitude of our family is one of moving closer to a shared core of spirituality.

30. We expect and allow our children to change as they move from age to age. We respect their fads, friends, confidences, privacy, and time—their right to be alone and their right to be different—as long as these things are not destructive.[2]

7

PLAY IS NECESSARY FOR A CLOSE-KNIT FAMILY

Seventeen years is a long time to know someone, and Ron's parents thought they knew him. What had happened during the previous summer, though, Ron's parents had no idea. All they knew was that when school began, their "normal," straight-A son had become a "punker." Black was the only color he would wear—a black Metallica T-shirt, black pants, black motorcycle boots—and with his earring-adorned ears (seven earrings total), shaved head, and obsession with heavy metal music, the seventeen-year-old Ron showed very little resemblance to the sixteen-year-old version. Mom and Dad were worried. Home had become a war zone. Each day when they came home from work they'd have to storm downstairs to Ron's locked bedroom, where the music was so loud the walls were shaking. They would bang on the door and loudly ask Ron to turn down the music.

After six months of escalating tension, Ron's parents decided to get counseling before they lost their child. Many issues came to the surface and the process went on for many months, but one of the solutions the counselor suggested sounded so bizarre they were reluctant to try it. "When you both get home tonight," he advised, "go down to your son's room, bang on the door, and when he answers tell him to turn his music off and come upstairs because you both want to talk to him. When he finally saunters into the room with a chip on his shoulder and slumps into the kitchen chair with an attitude, look him square in the eyes and say, 'Ron, your mother and I are counting to one hundred. Now go hide.'"

When you love your son like these parents did, desperation combined with love will motivate you to try anything—even play. And one night that is what they did. Can you imagine the look on Ron's face? Can you imagine what Ron said to his friends the next day? "You guys are never going to guess what happened last night. I played hide-and-seek with my parents until three in the morning. I still can't find them." Ron didn't become a Republican or start listening to country and western music, but when his parents played hide-and-seek with him, they did break through the longstanding tension and began the long process of healing.[1]

THIS MAY SOUND LIKE AN OVERSIMPLIFICATION, but the family or marriage that isn't "working" is a family or marriage that isn't playing together. Play, humor, fun, and building lifelong traditions are essential traits of happy, healthy families. Certainly our children need to do their chores, and of course they need discipline with consistency, but what they also need desperately from their parents is a rousing game of hide-and-seek or a monthly Ping-Pong tournament.

The Perrys go out for ice cream every Monday night. The Daniel family has taken golf lessons together. The Blakes move all the furniture in the living room and play a family game of soccer. These are families that by no means are perfect, but they have figured out that families need a little fun to break the tension and stress of living together under the same roof.

For years our family has taken an annual camping trip. Interestingly enough, I'm not the one who votes for camping; it's my wife. When

Cathy was growing up her family camped, and it is her most favorite memory of her family even though as a teenager she complained. With no offense to the female gender—or maybe it's just all the women in my life—as the only male in the family, camping is an interesting experience. Unpacking is always an event. "Rebecca, why did you bring your curling iron? There are no plugs." "Heidi, that's a cute dress, but do you think the bears will really care?" "Christy, I know outhouses are gross, but, yes, you will need to relieve yourself during this week so get over it!" As a loyal husband I won't tell you Cathy's stories, but it has something to do with driving eighty-seven miles to find a Starbucks while camping.

When the kids were younger, it was easier. Now camping is more difficult. They are not as excited about spending a week sleeping in a tent. They don't want to leave their friends. They don't like sleeping on the ground. They don't like the food. But Cathy and I just say, "We are going anyway, and don't forget to pack your swimsuit."

A funny thing takes place in the van as we always stop at our favorite fast-food place, In-N-Out Burger. The kids begin to leave home behind and, although they wouldn't always admit it, they enjoy each other's company. By the time we are at the camping spot, they turn a bit grumpy again. After we set up camp, light the fire, eat s'mores, and bring out some of the camping games that we haven't seen for a year, they forget that their blow-dryers don't work.

Every day, Cathy, the activities director, has something special planned for our family. Many days we complain about it, but by the end of the experience, we have to admit it was fun. Then there is always splurge day. That means we rent a Jet Ski or go whitewater rafting or take a bike trip to a beautiful lake or go out for a nice dinner. A funny thing happens on those camping trips: We begin to talk and laugh and lighten up. Family memories are built, inside jokes are shared, and serious moments of intimacy are communicated. There are low points too, just like in our regular weeks. But at the end of the year, usually between Christmas and New Year's, we take time to reflect on the year. You know what always pops up on the list of top three family experiences? It's the camping trip. Why? Because families need special times together to build lifelong memories and play together.

WHY PLAY?

As most experts on the family will say, a family that prays together stays together. But I would add that a family who consciously plays together will also be much more happy and healthy. For many families, play is the missing ingredient that will be the glue to hold the family together. Play heals closed spirits and brings broken marriages back together. As postmodern author Leonard Sweet puts it, "For a marriage to sing and dance, for two people to make beautiful music together, they need to play, not work, at their marriage."[2] Of course there is work involved to make a marriage strong or to parent with positive results, but for a family to really thrive, don't forget to ask the question, "Are we having fun yet?"

Play builds family memories. Have you ever noticed at extended family gatherings that much of the conversation is about past family experiences? "Do you remember the time Grandpa fell in the lake when we were fishing?" "I will never forget the trip we took to Disneyland." At a recent gathering of youth workers and their spouses, Cathy and I asked a purposely vague question, "What are a few of your family memories?" A minority of people in the group brought up negative memories about a divorce or another trauma in the home, but by far, most of them brought up memories centered on a time their family played together. Many of the memories were about trips their family took. We were amazed at how many of them were not about amusement parks, but rather times together camping, traveling, fishing with Grandpa—times centered on the outdoors and fun.

When my friend Tic Long goes on a trip, his family has a motto: "No bad food, no wrong turns, and no bad decisions." Basically what he is saying is cut loose, relax, and enjoy each other's company more than care about the details of the trip. The point is to go on trips, play together, and build memories—big memories and small memories. A healthy family takes time to play. Sure, it takes energy to make those memories happen, but it's worth it in our day and age, when there is so much stress and pressure in the family.

Play reduces family stress and tension. You are overstressed if you

- experience a continual sense of urgency and hurry or have no time to release and relax,

- have an underlying tension that causes a lot of sharp words, sibling quarrels, and marital misunderstandings,

- are preoccupied with escape, finding peace, going on vacation, quitting work, or family relationships,

- constantly feel frustration about getting things done, or

- have a nagging desire to find a simpler life.

None of these factors are unhealthy in and of themselves, but when you add them together and experience them for an extended period of time, then it is time to put away your work and responsibilities and take at least an eight-day "do nothing but play" vacation and find some perspective. The European culture is much healthier than the American culture when it comes to taking vacations. The average European takes almost twice as many days off from work a year than the average American. How crazy it is to raise your blood pressure to dangerous heights and work your fingers to the bones, to be overcommitted and fatigued most days, and then try to recuperate with a two-week vacation, only to go right back to the grind. Something tells all of us deep down in our hearts that something is terribly wrong with our lifestyle choices. So lighten up and figure out a way to reduce your family's stress and tension. If you can't find eight days to relax and lighten up, take five; if you can't find five days, then take two days; if you can't find two days, see a counselor because you are either on the road to burnout or your life and family are already a mess.

Play produces affirmation and support. We know instinctively that play produces family togetherness and support. We know that when we play together we have a deeper sense of belonging and community in the family. Parents must proactively work at making a sense of belonging and community one of the key goals of family togetherness. Here's a diagram that helps us understand the steps to family togetherness:

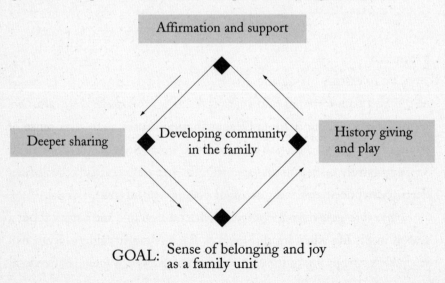

124

With the goal in mind of the family feeling a sense of belonging and joy, we can approach family togetherness with a reminder that first base is family history sharing and play. This could be sharing a family outing to Disneyland or interviewing grandparents on what it was like to grow up on a farm. Common history sharing is a first step to feeling a deeper sense of community in the family. Affirmation and support are key ingredients also. With busy families and sibling rivalries, a proactive time of affirmation makes a big difference.

One of our traditions is to play the game "affirmation bombardment" on a family member's birthday. At a special dinner prepared in their honor, we take a few moments and share at least three affirming thoughts each about our birthday family member. This means I know that at least once during the year something nice is going to be said to each sibling. When we start affirmation bombardment the kids usually roll their eyes, but every time before we are finished, the power of affirmation and support digs deep and becomes meaningful. Parents must look for ways for the family to express affirmation and support at all times, whether through something as simple as attending each other's activities or through more formalized activities like affirmation bombardment.

Out of history giving and affirmation comes a deeper sharing. Some of the best conversations and sharing of our souls happen only after we have invested in family time. Deeper sharing causes a stronger sense of community and a more powerful sense of belonging within the family. When a family opens up and shares on an intimate level, they will fill a deep-rooted need and feel a sense of belonging and joy.

Play causes good communication. My friend Bob told me a story about a season in his life when he and his son, Ryan, were struggling. Ryan had reached the magic age of thirteen, copped an attitude, wanted his freedom, and moved his dad from the top of his respect list to somewhere right below math word problems and just above doing his chores. The one thing they still had in common was a love for basketball. Bob made two very good decisions to keep the communication lines open. He bought two season tickets for the local university basketball team for his son and himself. Then he went to the local Wal-Mart and brought home a basketball hoop for the driveway. Between watching university basketball games together and almost daily playing one or two games of basketball together, Ryan and his dad kept improving the communication lines.

Bob, who is a pastor, told me that for most of the year his son showed little to no interest in attending their church. About the same time Dad had been demoted from the son's list, so had God. My friend was obviously concerned and had tried sitting his son down after dinner several times to have a formal talk about God. But, as Bob phrased it, "My son blew me off every time." Then one day in the middle of a particularly competitive game between father and son, Ryan stopped playing, looked at Bob, and asked, "Dad, do you think God could love a guy like me?" Bob smiled and said, "Yes, I do think God can love a guy like you, Ryan. Now take the ball out, and we can finish this conversation after I beat you this game." Bob called to tell me that after the game, father and son sat on the driveway and talked for an hour about spiritual issues. Bob was able to pray with his son to make a life-changing commitment to Christ. When I asked Bob who won the game, he said, "I don't remember!"

Why is it that most of our finest conversations do not take place when we sit our children down for a big talk? Spontaneous communication is almost always better because it is a deposit in your child's emotional bank account. Usually the best mutual exchanges take place on a walk, playing a game, eating ice cream, or doing anything fun or out of the ordinary.

Educators call this "hidden curriculum." It's almost always what takes place outside the classroom that is the best learning experience.

Playing together as a family may open up the communication process better than anything else you may try. So it may be time to be proactive and create those family fun days and events that provide the catalyst for more effective communication. Do whatever it takes to keep the communication lines open, even if it means picking up a basketball or going to the park on a regular basis. Don't forget that playing together and having a good time just may be the safety net you are hoping for to make a difference in your child's life.

HUMOR AND THE FAMILY

A friend of mine once said, "Family jokes, though rightly cursed by strangers, are the bond that keeps most families alive." Our family has favorite funny stories about our trips that crack us up every time but can't be translated to others because "you had to be there" to get the full meaning of the story. Humor heals broken families.

One of Cathy and my goals this year is to bring more comic relief to our family. With three active teenage girls in our family, life can get too intense. All five of us are strong-willed, and sometimes we just take life too seriously. I wrote a note on the refrigerator for me that simply says, "Lighten up!" We are making it a habit to rent classic comedy videos. Once or twice a year as a family we rent certain family favorites. When I travel, I ask Heidi to give me a joke of the day. When the family laughs together, we build a stronger bond.

Laughter is great medicine for any family. Did you know that the peak age of laughter is four? Four-year-olds laugh every four minutes or more than four hundred times a day. Adults laugh only fifteen times in an entire day. When Norman Cousins wrote the book *Anatomy of an Illness,* his premise was that humor and laughter have the power even to cure an illness—cancer, in his experience. If humor can cure an illness, then it definitely can have the power to bring families together.

TRADITIONS AND THE FAMILY

Some of our previous generations did a better job than we do with building family traditions. As I mentioned before, when the extended family gets together for a holiday, much of the conversation is centered around family traditions and family stories. We tell many of the same stories year after year at those gatherings. Traditions are important to impact the family. Planning and prioritizing make play and traditions happen. If we wait to have traditions just appear, they simply won't happen. You have to make it work for your family.

Here are some ideas:

Family fun nights. These are monthly times the family comes together to have fun. You can do the regulars like movies, dinner, or picnics, or you can be more creative and make up your own traditions and family fun times.

One-on-one times. We call these "dates" in our home. These are the times Rebecca and I go out for Mexican food or Christy and I take in a play or Heidi takes me surfing. I find that some of my most fruitful conversations with the girls happen during our monthly one-on-one times.

Service projects or mission trips. Many families draw closer together and get strength from serving together. Our church sponsors family mission trips to Mexico and Ecuador. Families come back glowing. Serving together can be just the experience to develop an even stronger family bond. Our family regularly visits a local rest home and women's shelter. These trips are worth the energy and effort.

Holiday traditions. Holidays can be stressful, but if you build in special family events that become traditions, you will be developing lifelong positive memories. Fifteen years ago, we noticed that a few people from our church had nowhere to go on Christmas Eve, so we spontaneously invited them to our home after the Christmas Eve service. On the way home I called a Chinese restaurant and ordered takeout. Every year since that time we have people over on Christmas Eve, and we always order Chinese takeout. We asked our girls this past year if we should change what we eat. They were insulted!

Adventures and vacations. You don't have to be rich to create great family vacations and adventures. Our kids know that every Easter vacation we will go to the beach, just like they know that each child gets to choose a family adventure when she graduates from high school.

COMMITTING TO PLAY

Todd Dean is one of my heroes. I've known him much of my adult life. He is a talented person with an MBA from Stanford University. Todd was a gymnast at the university, and when I met him, he was teaching students from my youth group to do a standing backflip. All I could think about was liability, and yet the kids loved watching him do his incredible flips. He invited me to try a backflip. I made a fool of myself, but he was still encouraging.

Todd married Charlotte. They had two beautiful children, and he had a very high-paying job. Todd's career was shooting through the roof.

Then tragedy struck, and Charlotte died of a brain tumor. Before Charlotte died, Todd had told me he wanted to coach his children's Little League and soccer teams. Because Todd's career expected some travel, he had to make some difficult decisions about his career. Todd was making good money, but it wasn't as important as playing catch with his son or rollerblading with his daughter.

Todd made the decision to quit his high-paying job and become a professor so he could play more with his kids and coach those teams. His salary was cut to what was once his expense account. His lifestyle changed with the salary cut. He doesn't live in as nice of a house as he could have, and his car isn't the same model as some of his other Stanford MBA friends, but he is happily coaching his children's teams. He is remarried to a lovely woman named Becky who had a similar loss story, and they have four happy, contented, and well-adjusted children who play and interact daily with their dad and mom, who sacrificed financially to help their family thrive. The benefits of playing together are far more valuable than a bigger paycheck.

FURTHER READING

- Yaconelli, Michael. *Dangerous Wonder: The Adventure of Childlike Faith*. Colorado Springs: NavPress, 1998.

DISCUSSION STARTERS

1. What fun family traditions do you remember as a child? What made them special?

2. What are some of your family's favorite things to do together?

3. Have you had any experiences where playing together brought about communication with a family member? What was it?

4. What can you plan this month as a special time for the family?

5. How can the following scripture apply to your family times together?

And whatever you do, whether in word or deed, do it all in the name of the Lord Jesus, giving thanks to God the Father through him. (Col. 3:17)

8

LOVE
YOUR SPOUSE

The more a marriage is spirited and sporting, the better off for the kids. It's impossible to have a healthy family without a healthy marriage. One of the best gifts parents can bequeath to children is the example of two people in love bound together in a vibrant covenant relationship.[1]

IT HAS OFTEN BEEN SAID that the best thing you can do for your children is to love your spouse. Sometimes that means putting your spouse's needs in front of your children's. A quality marriage is perhaps the optimum factor for rearing secure children. Many children who grew up in a home where the parents had a child-focused marriage say they have a difficult time knowing what exactly a good marriage looks like. In other words, your greatest family investment may be your marriage. If you are single, I'll get to you at the end of this chapter, but for now, know that you can have happy, healthy children even though it may be more difficult. The reason some single parents became single parents is that they didn't focus on their marriage during a season when it needed attention.

Cathy and I have what we call a "high-maintenance" marriage. We met the first day of college and were married one week after Cathy graduated from college. Our courtship and engagement were relatively uneventful when it came to conflict, but from the moment we arrived home after a wonderful honeymoon, we began to have a great amount of conflict. As a pastor doing youth ministry in a church, I remember having intense arguments with Cathy on the way to our youth group meeting and then standing up in front of the kids, feeling like a hypocrite. What made things worse was during that season in the church, people didn't talk much about marital conflict, so I thought we were the only ones out there with problems. I remember so well when one leader in our congregation told us that he and his wife had never had a fight. Never! My reaction was a deep sense of guilt. Yet, years later I now feel deeply sorry for them. Conflict and intimacy tend to go hand in hand.

OUR STORY

Perhaps our greatest marriage lesson came about five years into our union. After a year of marital unbliss we moved from California to Princeton, New Jersey, for graduate school. The Princeton years were actually better than our first year of marriage, but we still needed improvement. We both realized we didn't have the communication tools to work on our high-maintenance marriage, and yet we did have the desire.

After graduate school, we moved to Orange, California, where Cathy started teaching and I began a youth ministry program at a church. We became very busy. Cathy worked as a teacher by day and was my number one adult volunteer for the youth group by night. Our days, nights, mornings, and evenings were a blur of activity with the youth group. Our youth ministry grew from four kids on the first Sunday to more than one hundred in just three months, and the numbers just kept on growing. With numerical growth came loads of affirmation for me. After the first year the church actually doubled my salary. We counted that as at least as great a miracle as Jesus walking on water! We bought our first house and I thought life was going great. My entire being was focused on my work, which definitely gave me enthusiasm and self-esteem.

One night after a particularly excellent evening with the students, Cathy said, "Jim, we need to talk." I could see she was very serious, but being the dense male that I can be, I thought she wanted to talk about a problem with one of the kids in the youth group. At the time we were basically running a MASH unit for kids and families in crisis. "Helping families succeed" was my theme, and by the number of people participating in our program, we were prospering. Now Cathy and I were sitting across from each other at the Salt and Pepper Restaurant, open twenty-four hours a day.

"Jim, I feel abandoned by you. I feel resentment every time the phone rings or you are gone one more night. I know how you will probably respond, and you are partly right—God has been doing a special work in our ministry. But, Jim, I'm even beginning to resent God."

Cathy had me pegged. Yes, we were gloriously out of control but with all good things. It's true there had been little focus on our marriage, and intimacy was ebbing. I would come home after a very busy, successful, and stressful day and crash, only to get up and do it all over again the next day. Cathy went on to say, " I feel like you are having an affair. I can't imagine how you would find the time, but you sure aren't investing in our relationship."

I knew she was right. Cathy had even taken away my ammunition; I couldn't blame it all on God who was blessing our youth ministry. So I just said, "You're right. Not about the affair, but about the focus not being on our marriage."

Neither of us had very good role models in our lives in the areas of courtship, intimacy, and healthy relationships. We spent the next hour trying to figure out what to do. Was it time to quit my beloved work? How could we have the children we wanted with this kind of a lifestyle and this kind of a pace? We were embarrassed to talk with anyone and really share how bad it was. In the midst of our immaturity and lack of knowledge, we came up with three action steps that proved to be lifesavers for our marriage and good boundaries when children showed up in our lives.

Sitting at the table in the restaurant we wrote on a napkin:

1. Non-negotiable date night

2. Only out three nights a week

3. Cathy to have veto power over the schedule

These three decisions were our action steps. I looked forward to the date night idea, but I didn't know how we would find the time. The decision to work toward only being out working three nights a week felt awfully oppressive, but I knew I needed to take a drastic measure. And the veto power over the schedule was almost a passive-aggressive act on my part to appease Cathy's concerns. I saw it as a bit of an overreaction to her critique of our marriage. And yet, those three decisions became the lifeline to a healthier relationship and a foundation for making better decisions as children came into our life.

DO YOU HAVE A NON-NEGOTIABLE DATE NIGHT?

Cathy and I don't miss many date nights. We know that even though life can get overly busy and we often get distracted, at least once a week, we are going to stop what we are doing and focus on each other. Most of our dates aren't very expensive. In fact, when our children were younger, the cost of a baby-sitter was sometimes more expensive than the date. The date is not a time to talk about the bills or the kids' school plans; it is a time to focus on each other. It's not a time to let down, but a time to pour some positive deposits in the direction of your spouse.

Last year when Cathy and I celebrated our twenty-fifth wedding anniversary, sent the kids to camp, and took a very special trip, we spent much of our time talking about the kids. We were actually glad to be away from the kids, knowing they were safe and having a good time, but still so much of our focus was on them. This is fine. Unless you wake up one day and realize you have nothing in common with your spouse except for the kids and that one or both of you have given all their energy to other priorities and not to each other. Cathy can handle a busy schedule as long as she knows that there will be a sanctuary of love, support, and focus on our weekly date night. (Date mornings and date afternoons are good too.)

HOW MANY NIGHTS A WEEK IS YOUR FAMILY HOME TOGETHER?

We decided to be out only three nights each week. There is nothing magical about the number three; it just works for us. The average pastor in America is out five nights a week. Cathy and I can't function as well with that much time away from home. You have to learn what works for you as a couple and family and then make decisions to constantly bring health and renewal to the relationship.

Last week, one of Rebecca's fourteen-year-old friends was over for dinner before youth group. We sat down at the table for a rushed meal, but we were all together. Her friend commented, "This is so nice. I can't remember the last time our family sat around the kitchen table for dinner!" Interestingly enough, the girl's mother had just confided to Cathy and me that life was extremely difficult at home. A few more nights a week together won't necessarily take away all your problems, but this discipline has been a godsend for our family.

DOES YOUR SPOUSE HAVE VETO POWER OVER YOUR SCHEDULE?

With our line of work, the calendar is one of our biggest nightmares and bones of contention. When I first gave Cathy veto power over my schedule, I only saw it as a control agent for her and a negative for me. I was wrong. Some of our most intense disagreements were about the schedule that Cathy had not bought into. Today we do the calendar together, and we seldom if ever argue or blame each other about it. There are times we grieve together our decisions that brought a hectic time into our life, but because we both made the decision it's easier not to blame the other person. Cathy tends to be more aware of the details of the family schedule. I have a tendency to say yes to everything, and she guards me from me.

IS THE SPARK STILL THERE?

Over time in every relationship, a couple's life can become predictable. Romance, sex, and even conversation can become routine or nonexistent. If "routine" or "predictable" sum up your situation, then it's time to refocus some of your energy on your spouse. When your relationship is suffering due to lack of attention, here are some questions to help you evaluate what needs to happen to light the spark again:

1. Before you were married, when you and your spouse were dating, what did you do to make him or her feel special?

2. What are you doing right now to make your mate feel special?

3. What was the last fun activity you and your spouse did together?

4. How often do you participate in activities you both enjoy?

5. If you asked your spouse to list your top five priorities based on where you devote the most time and effort, what would those priorities be?

6. Where does your spouse rank on that list?

These questions might be a good start to get the dialogue moving in the right direction and keep the spark burning brighter than ever.

Most of the couples I know tell me that they love each other, but they are just too busy with their work, kids, and all the other activities they are juggling. All of their time is focused on good things, but they have let their marriage slide a bit and hope to make some changes in the near future. Now is the time to make the important decisions.

Ron and Susan are the perfect illustration of a couple who mean well but have discovered that their marriage is suffering because they are just too busy. Ron is a policeman. Susan is a preschool teacher. She teaches because they need the money, but it also works well with their three children's schedules. Ron told me they literally put all of their schedules on a computer. With soccer, ballet, school, church, jobs, music lessons, and much more, their life is pretty complicated. By the time the kids get to bed, Ron and Susan are too tired to relate to each other; and when they are tired and stressed, they tend to argue more than relate. Ron's replenishing relationships are with his fellow police officers, and Susan gets her support from her mother, who lives in another city, and a couple of the teachers from her school.

They confided in me that although things looked great on the outside, they were very worried that their marriage was crumbling from the inside out. I asked what I thought was a simple question: "What areas of your busy life can you cut back on and refocus your energy on each other?"

They went through a litany of activities that would make anyone tired. They concluded with, "There is absolutely nothing we can change."

"What about jobs?" I asked.

"We need the money," they insisted.

"What about all the kids' activities?" I continued.

"We can't change a thing. Neither of us had the opportunity to do all this stuff, and we want our kids to enjoy any activity they can."

I had to tell them the painful truth. "Then it looks like those beautiful, busy kids of yours will be excellent soccer players and musicians but have parents who don't like each other very much." They didn't enjoy my comment.

The answer for Ron and Susan, and maybe you, is cut back and do less. To find the time to replenish your relationship, you might need to cut something out of your busy schedule. Can I let you in on a secret? Kids would rather have parents who like each other than learn one more musical instrument or score another goal in soccer. I'm not telling you to back off completely, but just find a rhythm for your family that works for everyone including the marriage equation.

LET THE ROMANCE BEGIN . . . OR CONTINUE

There is a significant drop in satisfaction with a couple's romance and sex lives when children arrive on the scene. However, couples with the most positive families make sex and romance a priority. Don't let kids, money, busyness, or anything else rob you of romance. When I kiss Cathy in front of my kids, they act like they are grossed out but they like it. It gives them security. The only way to make romance a priority is to schedule it onto the calendar. Sure a scheduled date night is not as spontaneous as before you had children, but if you don't schedule in special times together, they probably won't happen enough.

Two scripture verses from the New Testament are meaningful to me in this area. Ephesians 5:25 says, "Love your wives." The actual Greek meaning is "Keep on loving (or even treasuring) your wives." This goes for wives also. The other verse is not just about marriage, but it is one of the foundation verses for our marriage: "Outdo one another in showing honor" (Rom. 12:10 NRSV). When we try to treat our spouse as a king or queen, it shows them we care. Cathy likes to say, "Romance starts in the morning with how we treat each other through the day."

KEEP GROWING SPIRITUALLY

Here's an interesting observation. Never in all my years of youth and family ministry and counseling couples have I ever encountered a couple experiencing serious difficulties who were praying together. Nor have I ever known a couple who, once they had agreed to pray together and stuck to it, ended up getting a divorce. Praying together restores balance and priorities in a marriage because it recognizes that God loves both partners equally. Furthermore, bringing a disagreement before the bar of ultimate justice removes it somehow from human bitterness. People change their tone of voice, and it becomes almost impossible to remain argumentative.

Marriage experts Les and Leslie Parrott report a recent study showed that couples who attend church, even as little as once a month, increase their chances of staying married for life. Studies also show that church-goers feel better about their marriages than those who don't worship together. Research shows that the happiest couples are those who pray together. Couples who pray together are twice as likely as those who don't pray together to describe their marriages as being highly romantic. And according to the Parrotts, married couples who pray together are 90 percent more likely to report higher satisfaction with their sex lives than couples who don't pray together. Prayer draws couples and families closer together. It's like the young couple who decided to start their honeymoon by kneeling beside their bed to pray. The bride giggled when she heard her new husband's prayer: "For what we are about to receive, may the Lord make us truly thankful!"

One of the common themes in the temptation narratives of the Bible is isolation. That's why for Cathy and my spiritual betterment and growth as a couple we choose to be in a regular couples' Bible study as well as our own same-sex support groups. Who replenishes your relationships spiritually? Are you proactively seeking out mentors to help you grow spiritually as a marriage partner and as an individual? Do you have a regular daily time with God in prayer and devotion? Do you ever take time as a couple to participate in a couples' retreat at your church or one of the many programs offered around the country to enhance your marriage and your spiritual life?

KEEP ON COMMUNICATING

Cathy and I do not feel that we had excellent role models when it came to communicating as we were growing up. We have inherited some of the same poor habits of our parents and even grandparents. We've laughed that if my father and Cathy's mother were to get married, it would be the beginning of World War III. And then we pause for a moment and realize that in many ways, when it comes to communication styles, they did get married, in us!

When Cathy and I were first married, we made the mistake of never discussing the topic of finances. I assumed that I would handle them; after all, my father never allowed my mother to touch the checkbook. On the other hand, Cathy's mom handled the finances in her home, and she expected to do the same. Cathy is a detail person. The bank statement must balance to the penny even if it takes her all night. I am much more comfortable rounding most everything off to the nearest ten dollars and moving on to something more fun. You can imagine the conflict that started when "her mom" and "my dad" met over the finances. It wasn't a pretty sight. Cathy would get upset, and I would get my feelings hurt; then we would move from finances to anything else that was bugging us. Before we knew it neither of us liked each other very much anymore.

How does a high-maintenance marriage with poor communication skills like ours survive? You have to work at it almost every day. As you work on your communication skills, not only are you assuring your marriage's success, but you are also role modeling for your children how to communicate so their future relationships will have a better chance as well. Here are a few rules that work for us.

"After 10:30 P.M." rule. I get up early. Cathy is a night owl. I'm the guy who one night while praying together as a couple fell asleep in the middle of my own prayer! By default Cathy always has the advantage in conflicts after 10:30 P.M., and I will automatically win the battle before 8:00 A.M. We know that for good communication or conflict resolution to take place, we do better before 10:30 P.M. and not in the middle of the pit hours of preparation for dinner, homework, bedtime for the kids, and all the other things that we have to face between 6:00 P.M. and 9:00 P.M. We also know it is almost worthless to communicate before our kids go to school. These boundaries and expectations help us find times when we can focus on each other and are in a better place and frame of reference.

"It's more difficult in bed" rule. In my opinion, the marriage bed is sacred; it's for sleeping and, uh, you know. If Cathy and I need to meet about the kids or discuss a potential conflict, we have not found the bed to be the place most conducive to communication. I fall asleep, and that makes Cathy frustrated. We have found that if we regularly schedule a "Burns Family Business Meeting," we can use that time to take care of the business-type issues of the family. This is where we try to discuss the schedule, insurance problems, finances, car needs, house needs, and all the rest of the stuff it takes to run a family.

Most couples do not have a set time each week to meet, so the "business issues" are often put off or brought up at an inappropriate time or place. I don't know about you, but the weekly business meeting isn't my favorite time with my spouse. However, it is one of our most important hours of the week, and it keeps us from having to deal with the business issues on our date night or during our times of spiritual growth together or on the run.

"Take your temperature before you have a fever" rule. You might call this rule the "preventative medicine" rule. Do you and your spouse schedule in times of extended communication to take a longer look at the needs of your marriage and family life? Dave and Pam Hicks have four absolutely incredible adult daughters. One of their daughters, Carrie, works as my assistant, so I have firsthand knowledge that they did a magnificent job! Years ago Dave and Pam told Cathy and me one of their secrets to a healthy family life. Every six months while their children were growing up, they would go away for the day or overnight when possible. They would talk about each child one at a time and discuss what they hoped to work on for the next six months in that child's life. They would write down their decisions and then review them during the next six-month period. That's proactive parenting: focusing on prevention rather than allowing the rearing of your children to happen by chance.

Cathy and I make a habit of going away for a few days right around our anniversary and not only celebrating the year, but also evaluating our marriage. Some years it's been a wonderful exercise in positive communication, and other times we've had to ask, "How did we get through this year still liking each other?"

A couple of memorable times come to mind. One year Cathy planned the whole trip. It was just one night away, but we really needed it. She enjoyed surprising me with an overnight at a bed-and-breakfast overlooking beautiful Lake Arrowhead in the Southern California mountains. We had a great dinner and a great night.

Cathy didn't want to be distracted, so after we checked out the bed-and-breakfast, she rented a rowboat. As we sat in the middle of the lake, she handed me a sheet she had prepared from a book she had been reading called *His Needs, Her Needs,* which discusses key needs of a wife and a husband. The sheet of paper Cathy gave me had ten needs of couples listed. She asked me to rank in order from most important to least important what I thought would be her needs and then write down how I would rank my own needs on the other side of the page. Three hours later we were still discussing how to meet each other's needs more effectively. You may want to borrow the same idea.

His Needs/Her Needs[2]

- Sexual fulfillment
- Recreational companionship
- An attractive spouse
- Domestic support
- Admiration
- Affection
- Conversation
- Honesty and openness
- Financial support
- Family commitment

A strong marriage definitely takes a great deal of work. However, the results are well worth it when you look at the vitality it brings to your entire family. Is your marriage a child-focused marriage? Marriages that are totally child-focused don't work well and, most of the time, don't last. Your children want and need you to invest time and effort into your marriage. Even if they complain about date nights or extended times away for you and your spouse, in their hearts they know that you and your spouse need time alone.

A good marriage will bring much security to a child. If it has been a while since you and your spouse took the time to focus on each other instead of the kids, then don't delay. Now is the time to put the needs of the kids aside for a brief period and rekindle the emotional, physical, and spiritual bond that once burned brightly for you and your spouse.

A WORD TO SINGLE PARENTS

If you are a single parent and you have stayed with me through this chapter, then you probably have some mixed feelings about the content. Just a few weeks ago I spoke to our single parents' group at our church, and I was once again reminded of what incredible people single parents are and the extra load they carry. Parenting is tough enough with two people, let alone with one.

As I looked out at this group of very tired but diligent single parents, I shared with them a story from the Bible. Moses and the Israelites were battling their archenemy, the Amalekites. God instructed Moses to hold his arms up high above his head with his staff in his hand. When Moses kept his arms raised, the Israelites would begin winning the battle; but when he grew tired and he dropped his arms, the Amalekites would start winning the battle. Finally an exhausted Moses asked others to stand beside him and help keep his arms held high by literally holding his arms in place. The Israelites ended up winning the battle because of the helpers Moses used to keep his arms held high.

I asked these wonderful people in the single parent group, "Who comes alongside you to help you with your children when you get tired or lose perspective along the way?" I ended up putting my notes away, and for the rest of the evening, this was our discussion. In general, this group was discouraged and too tired to fight some of the battles that needed fighting. Our general consensus was that *all* parents, but especially single parents, have to find the stamina to ask for help and find replenishing relationships for themselves and their children. The church is a very good place to seek out some of those replenishing relationships.

I told them about our friend Mary, who is a single parent and my pick for "Mother of the Year." She is a networker. She finds others whom she can serve and who can serve her family needs. She has chosen to be involved in her church, where many of the moms take care of each other and look after the needs of each other's children. She can't afford fancy vacations or even much time off from work, but she still manages to create family fun nights and vacation traditions on a shoestring budget that will make wonderful memories for her children. Her life didn't turn out the way she had dreamed it would, but she is constantly on the lookout for ways to focus on the positive as well as find people like her church youth workers who can help her bring up her children to one day be responsible adults. No one said it would be easy, but with God's help and finding the right people to come alongside you, your kids will thrive.

FURTHER READING

- Chapman, Gary. *The Five Love Languages: How to Express Heartfelt Commitment to Your Mate.* Chicago: Northfield Publishing, 1992.

- Smalley, Gary. *Making Love Last Forever.* Nashville: Word, 1997.

- Willard F. Harley Jr. *His Needs, Her Needs*. Grand Rapids: Fleming H. Revell, 1988.

DISCUSSION STARTERS

1. Were your parents positive or negative role models for a healthy marriage?

2. Do you agree or disagree with the following statement from Billy Graham?

   "If couples would put half the effort into marriage that they put into courtship, they would be surprised how things would brighten up."

3. Which areas of your marriage need improving? Which areas are doing well?

4. How does the following scripture apply to your marriage?

   Submit to one another out of reverence for Christ. (Eph. 5:21)

5. For further conversations, read Ephesians 5:22–33. Discuss the concept of submission to each other and submission to God.

Here are other communication tools that have worked for us.

COMMUNICATION QUESTIONS AND ISSUES

Discuss each area below with your spouse topic by topic.
  A. Issues
      Goals, thoughts, worries, hopes, and dreams
      Our relationship
      The ministry
      Spiritual
      Sex
      Family
          • Children
          • In-laws
          • Each other
      Financial
      Education
      Physical
      Spouse's needs
      Fears
      Other issues

  B. Complete These Sentences
      Sometimes I become blocked in our relationship when . . .
      Sometimes I feel angry when . . .
      Sometimes when I am happy, I . . .
      One of the things I wish you knew more about me is . . .
      If I could be sure no one would laugh at me . . .
      Ever since I was a child . . .

THE FIVE LANGUAGES OF LOVE[3]

- Words of affirmation
- Quality time
- Receiving gifts
- Acts of service
- Physical touch

1. What are your two primary languages of love?

2. What are your spouse's two primary languages of love?

3. Specify what you can do to give out love in your spouse's love language.

MAKING LOVE LAST FOREVER

Be sure you are making more deposits into your spouse's emotional well-being than withdrawals. A *deposit* is anything positive and security producing that gives your mate energy. A *withdrawal* is anything sad or negative that drains energy from your mate.

1. In what ways can you make more deposits into your spouse's account?

2. What deposits do you wish you could receive from your spouse?

3. Identify ways you are making withdrawals from your spouse's account.

9

THE BEST THINGS IN LIFE ARE NOT THINGS

Dear Dad,

$chool i$ really great. I am making lot$ of friend$ and $tudying very hard. With all my $tuff, I $imply can't think of anything I need, $o if you would like, you can ju$t $end me a card, a$ I would love to hear from you.

Love,

Your $on

Dear Son,

I kNOw that astroNOmy, ecoNOmics, and oceaNOgraphy are eNOugh to keep even an hoNOr student busy. Do NOt forget that the pursuit of kNOwledge is a NOble task, and you can never study eNOugh.

Love,

Dad

FOR SEVERAL YEARS CATHY AND I have given our daughters money each semester for a clothes allowance. With this income they may choose to buy whatever clothing they want (within reason), but it is all the money they will receive for clothes for the semester. Christy has it figured out. She looks for sales and is quite the bargain shopper. On the other hand, Rebecca chooses more expensive clothes and shops at the spur of the moment. In our family Christy shops like Mom and Rebecca shops like Dad! Last week I saw Christy wearing Rebecca's new expensive skirt that she had never worn. I asked if she had Rebecca's permission, and she told me Rebecca had sold it to her for half price. Why would she do that? Because Rebecca spent her entire clothing allowance and forgot to purchase shoes! She had asked Mom to bail her out. Mom offered a small loan, but Rebecca chose to sell her skirt to get new shoes. Rebecca learned a lesson that many kids don't learn until adulthood: There is only so much money to go around, and the decisions you make about how you spend will either benefit you or strap you and add more pressure than you want or need.

Let's face it. Money is a problem in families, and most of us do not have as much as we want. Families are often more focused on money problems than they would ever want to be. I think it is partly because of poor decisions and planning. Families with a huge weight of debt are families who struggle. Families who handle their money properly, whether they are rich, poor, or in-between, are much happier, healthier families. Money may not be able to buy you love, but it is one of the key issues of conflict in marriages and one of the missing topics when parenting for positive results. Perhaps the most sobering financial statistic of all is the fact that a Gallup poll found 56 percent of all divorces are the result of financial tension in the home!

When I worked in the church as a youth pastor, I realized people didn't like the pastor to speak about money. They would say it is private and personal. Jesus sure didn't have a problem talking about money. The Bible says a great deal about money. Authorities tell us that there are around 500 verses on prayer, 500 verses on faith, and more than 2,350 verses on money!

Whether we like it or not, much of our world and our family decisions revolve around money. This definitely doesn't mean that materialism is the answer to family problems. On the contrary, our focus on finances will be a major determining factor for helping our family succeed as well as the financial health and stewardship of our children and family. I have spent much of my life living in affluent areas of the country and yet some of the most unhealthy and unhappy families I have ever known come from neighborhoods with mortgages and lease payments that most of us can hardly imagine. This may not sound very politically correct, but some of the healthiest families I ever met were on the east coast of communist Cuba. These families live under an oppressed government, and their monthly income is fourteen dollars. Materially they have very little, but they have learned to live content and beautiful lives. They understand the spiritual concept of stewardship much better than some of my wealthier friends whose families are falling apart.

The decisions we make as parents about our financial health often play a major factor in our family's overall lifestyle. Jesus summarized it so well in the Sermon on the Mount when he said, "For where your treasure is, there your heart will be also" (Matt. 6:21). A few sentences later in that most incredible sermon, he went on to challenge his listeners with these words: "No one can serve two masters. Either he will hate the one and love the other, or he will be devoted to the one and despise the other. You cannot serve both God and Money" (v. 24).

Basically there are two economic systems battling for our family's soul. The world's value places emphasis on things and stuff. God's value is invested in people, stewardship, and beauty. The problem lies in the fact that the world system influences all of us; the balance of money and spirit is not only a problem for parents, but for children as well. According to

Jesus, we pay most of our attention to whatever we treasure. Our hearts are drawn to our treasure.

I like the perspective of a Catholic priest who was approached by thieves who came into his beautiful cathedral to steal some of its valuable treasures. With a gun pointed at the head of the priest, they said, "Show us your valuable treasures." He agreed. They walked into the cathedral, past the golden altar, and out the back door. He pointed to a group of twenty orphans playing ball in the back. He said, "These are the treasures of this cathedral."

Stewardship is a spiritual issue. Someone once said, "A man or woman can enrich his or her bank account at the expense of empowering his or her soul." Martin Luther once said, "You cannot be truly converted unless heart, mind, and *pocketbook* are converted." Isn't it true that the amount of light that gets into any room depends on the state of the window through which the light must pass? With this in mind, the light that gets into our soul depends on the spiritual state of our focus.

For many, what we focus on is what we become. I asked a group of teenagers what they wanted to be when they grew up. I received all kinds of answers: attorney, pastor, homemaker, teacher, businessperson. One fourteen-year-old, Jerry, simply said, "I want to be rich." "Okay, Jerry," I replied, "but what do you want to be? What kind of job? What do you want to do?" He shot right back, "You don't understand. I don't care what I do. I just want to be wealthy. I want a large home overlooking the water, with a boat and a Porsche." I came back at him and simply said, "I think your goals are too low. Success is not spelled M-O-N-E-Y." Unfortunately, Jerry's parents had planted into his brain the misconception that only wealthy people are happy. Sorry, Jerry; it's not as much about money as you have been taught.

WHAT ARE YOUR CHILDREN LEARNING BY THE WAY YOU HANDLE MONEY?

A family consumed with money problems is often a family who somewhere along the road made a wrong turn. As stated earlier, money issues are always one of the top reasons for divorce. Money problems reach up to the richest of the rich and also show up in pastors' homes. Money is on the minds of everyone on skid row as well as the financial district two blocks down the street.

Cathy and I don't always excel at stewardship. We, like most Christians, are trying. We are improving. Sometimes Cathy and I speak on ministry and marriage. We love ministry couples, but frankly, like ourselves, they often have to work extra hard to maintain a healthy marriage and family. When we speak, we almost always bring up the issue of finances. We only plan for a few minutes on this topic, but it never fails to become one of the major areas of interest for pastors and their spouses. Here's our simple outline.

Spend less than you make. When we first started speaking on finances, we actually threw that line in for comic relief. We thought they would laugh. They didn't. They got serious and wrote it down in their notes. Why? Because most Americans don't spend less than they make. At last count, individuals in America alone owe more than three trillion dollars. The average family spends four hundred dollars more than they earn each year. Personal consumer debt increases at the rate of one thousand dollars per second, and debt has now reached a level where 23 percent of the average person's take-home pay is already committed to payment of existing debt—and that is not including their home mortgage! We have so much personal debt in our country that the average person has been described as someone driving on a bond-financed highway, in a bank-financed car, fueled by charge-card-financed gasoline, going to purchase furniture on the installment plan to put in his savings-and-loan-financed home! The fact is we are drowning in a sea of debt, and we are bound to have serious financial, spiritual, and family casualties. However, there is an answer. Go against the grain of our culture and have the discipline to spend less than you make.

A budget is a must. In one of the most popular financial books of the previous decade, *The Millionaire Next Door,* the authors set out to find the millionaires in our country and document what they do and how they make their money. The authors were shocked at what they discovered. The millionaires didn't all live in the most expensive houses. They were people who lived fairly ordinary lives with a couple of key principles that brought them wealth. One of the principles was that they obviously spent less than they made, but the most common ingredient was they lived with a budget. If you don't have a budget, you cannot possibly know if you are winning or losing in the debt war. A budget is a map to help you stay on track with your finances and be a faithful steward of the resources God has given you.

Debt is slavery. Credit, interest, and debt are just poor stewardship. Del and Elaine buy two brand-new mountain bikes for $475 apiece. With taxes their investment is a little more than $1,000. They put their new purchase on a credit card that offers 18 percent interest. Two years later, they are still paying for the bikes they have ridden only twice, and now the cost is up to approximately $1,400. Here's what the Bible says about debt: "The rich rule over the poor, and the borrower is servant to the lender" (Prov. 22:7). With debt you literally become a slave to the lender. Deuteronomy 28:1–2 says: "If you fully obey the LORD your God and carefully follow all his commands I give you today, the LORD your God will set you high above all the nations on earth. All these blessings will come upon you and accompany you if you obey the LORD your God."

Debt even extracts a physical toll. Debt often increases stress, which contributes to mental, physical, and emotional fatigue that stifles creativity and harms relationships.

Delayed gratification is the answer. What would have been the better use of Del and Elaine's money? As much as they desired the bikes, they didn't have the cash to buy them, so they should have waited. They either could have developed a savings plan for the bikes, or "bike fever" would have gone away and now they would not be strapped with a huge bill and no place to put the bikes they seldom use. Children see; children do. If you ask a five-year-old if they would like a double-decker ice cream on a hot day or a fifty-dollar savings bond for college, which do you think they will take? No doubt the ice cream. However, after years of watching their parents make delayed gratification decisions, they will eventually begin to get it.

A young businessman was eager to learn from the founder of the company how to handle finances. He went to the wise old man and asked him, "Sir, could you tell me what it takes to become wise in the area of financial stewardship like you?"

The wise old businessman paused and said, "Certainly, my son—two words."

The young man said, "Please tell me, sir, what are those two words?"

The wise old man said, "Good decisions."

The young man thought about this and then said boldly, "Sir, can you tell me how you learn to make good decisions about finances?"

The wise old businessman thought for a second and said, "Certainly, my son, one word—experience."

The young man said, "Please, sir, permit me one more question. How do you get experience?"

The wise old businessman said, "Son, two words—bad decisions."

Give 10 percent of your income, and save 10 percent of your income. This may be an oversimplification, but I have never met anyone who consistently has tithed on their income and saved 10 percent of their income who has had a major financial problem. Back to the millionaires next door. They probably acquired their wealth through the miracle of compound interest and a drastic savings program. Hopefully these same people took seriously the biblical mandate of the tithe and applied it to their lives as well.

Several years ago I helped run the annual stewardship campaign for our church. It was an enlightening experience to say the least. Only a few of us read the "pledge cards," so for that season I was in the know of who gave what to the church. It was a most humbling experience. Some of the largest givers were by no means the wealthiest. However, as I looked at the families who were generous with their gifts, I noticed something else about them: They were many of the healthiest families in our congregation. If you don't currently have a savings plan, start small, but start this week. If you don't regularly give a percentage of your income back to God, then start today. It's a great reminder that all of your treasure comes from him anyway.

The answer to the money pit issue is to be a faithful steward of your resources. This is by far the most powerful way to teach children to be responsible with their resources now and as they grow up. It is never too early to introduce the biblical concept of stewardship to your children. Basically, as children move from dependence on us to independence, the lessons they learn about stewardship will help prepare them for adulthood in one of the most important ways possible. Financial counselor Ron Blue defines stewardship as, "The use of God-given resources for the accomplishment of God-given goals." Blue lists four principles to live by and teach our children:

1. God owns it all.
2. There is always a trade-off between time and effort and money and rewards.

3. There is no such thing as an "independent financial decision."

4. Delayed gratification is the key to financial maturity.[1]

I like what my father used to say: "The best things in life are not things!"

Howard Dayton is a friend and hero of mine who started a wonderful organization called Crown Ministries. Crown takes the concept of financial stewardship and trains thousands of men and women to be faithful and consistent with their financial resources. I have called them a "healing and deliverance" mission for the majority of people who need to be set free from financial bondage. Years ago, Howard created a "Faithful Steward" diagram that helps us keep the goal in mind. You can use the diagram below as a thermometer to gauge your own stewardship and as a goal to move toward. I keep this diagram close to my heart as I look at our own finances and the responsibility of training our children in this most important but overlooked area.

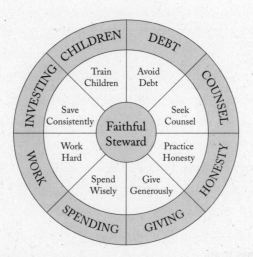

Take a look at each area of this diagram and rate how you are doing as a faithful steward of your finances. Next rank each area of the diagram from 1 to 5 below, and make a decision to improve where improvement is needed.

1	3	5
Needs immediate attention	so-so	not perfect but do a good job

Avoid debt _____

Seek counsel_____

Practice honesty_____

Give generously_____

Spend wisely _____

Work hard _____

Save consistently_____

Train children _____

TEACH YOUR CHILDREN ABOUT MONEY

If a family doesn't have a proactive training process for their children's morals and values, then they probably won't be doing much in the area of training their children to handle finances in a right way either. Just as when it comes to morals and values, many parents don't teach their children because they still have a great deal of work in this area also. So learn together. That's what our family has done.

Cathy and I realized that although we might receive higher marks on the stewardship report card with our personal finances than some people, we did not do a good job of training our children. It came to a head one day when our oldest was about seven years old and she thought all you had to do was go to the ATM machine and get money out if you needed something. She was shocked to hear that you actually had to put something in the bank first in order to get it out.

Here are a few questions to consider:

1. Does our family have a stewardship philosophy? Can our children articulate our family's stewardship agenda?

2. Do our children know the power of giving?

3. Do they understand the emptiness of materialism and the benefits of delayed gratification?

4. Have we given them charge of some area of their financial lives to teach them personal responsibility? (Obviously, this must be age-appropriate.)

Help your children develop a stewardship plan. If you haven't done much work with your children in this area, then there is no better time to start than now. What is your family's stewardship philosophy? One family we know discussed it with their kids and came up with this paragraph: "Our material possessions are actually on loan to us from God. We acknowledge his generous love and gifts to us. We will be a family who looks for ways to give generously, stays out of debt except for our house and car, and realizes that everything we have is on loan from God anyway." Another family borrowed a quote from somewhere: "When it comes to money small things are small things, but faithfulness with small things is a big thing." They went on to write, "We will faithfully look for ways to faithfully give back to God." Our family uses the diagram from Howard Dayton and then fills in specifics for our family in each of the areas and then we review the goals.

Consider your children's allowance to be payday. We like the idea of a regular payday. Some people give their children an allowance on the day they receive their paycheck. We tend to go weekly. The benefit of an allowance is that whatever the age of your child, they will learn something about personal responsibility as they learn to manage money for some of the things they need. We increase the allowance with responsibility for more purchases with age.

Guiding your children on the subject of money offers you as parents the opportunity to teach them stewardship and increases their sense of responsibility and self-reliance. Allowances are the first step in learning money management. Look at an allowance as a minisalary to help young people learn how to handle money. A good rule is that a small allowance begins when the child must learn some money management skills, which is usually around the time they go to school. As the children get older, give them more allowance for more responsibility; and by the time they leave the house, they should be handling almost all their purchases and budget.

Teach your children early to tithe and save. Most kids have trouble with the concepts of saving and tithing. Since so few American adults save and tithe, the concept isn't difficult just for kids! Find a bank with low or no-fee passbook accounts. Let them watch the interest grow. Establish some goals for savings, and help keep them accountable to meet their savings goals.

Cathy and I have not gone broke with our offer of matching dollar for dollar whatever our girls put in savings or giving. It is still a good way to encourage the power of giving and saving. We let our daughters help make decisions on some of our discretionary giving to charity, missions, and the church. Our kids sponsor two Compassion International children.[2] We have watched them grow up and mature. Our children write to their Compassion children and are excited when they receive letters back.

Help your children understand the positive power of a budget. Most couples who come to my office for premarital counseling are surprised when I tell them I will not meet with them again unless they show me a simple budget before the next session. Most of them have never put together a budget, and I usually have to coach them or offer them one of the many outstanding resources by Howard Dayton, Ron Blue, or Larry Burkett, to name a few of the excellent financial stewardship gurus today. You don't have to make the budget with your children complicated. In fact, the simpler the budget, the better. When your children are in elementary school, a budget may look as simple as giving/saving/spending. As they get older and you give them more financial responsibilities, you can add giving, saving, school activities, personal grooming, entertainment, clothing, and gifts. Asking your teenagers to create a monthly spending journal is a great addition to the budget as well.

MONTHLY JOURNAL

Month_____
Opening Balance: $47.50

DATE	DESCRIPTION	INCOME	EXPENSES	BALANCE
1/13	Allowance	3.00		50.50
1/15	Baby-sitting	10.00		60.50
1/16	Gift to the church		5.00	55.50
1/20	Movie and snacks		13.00	42.50
1/24	Gift from Aunt Ann	20.00		62.50
1/24	Makeup		3.50	59.00
1/28	Bowling		7.00	52.00
1/29	T-shirt		18.00	34.00
Closing Balance: $34.00				

Some of the greatest problems families face are centered on finances. As a youth worker, I have met many people who are from very well-off families whose children didn't learn about stewardship even though they had plenty of money. Money is spiritual. Money is worldly. How we handle our finances will greatly influence the direct fulfillment in our lives. I keep this piece entitled *Money and You* close to our family's heart:

> Money can buy medicine, but not health.
> Money can buy a house, but not a home.
> Money can buy companionship, but not a friend.
> Money can buy entertainment, but not happiness.
> Money can buy food, but not an appetite.
> Money can buy a bed, but not sleep.
> Money can buy a crucifix, but not a savior.
> Money can buy the good life, but not eternal life.
>
> —Author Unknown

FURTHER READING

- Blue, Ron, and Judy Blue. *Money Matters for Parents and Their Kids*. Nashville: Thomas Nelson, 1988.

- Blue, Ron. *Mastering Money in Your Marriage*. Loveland, Colo.: Group Publishing, 2000.

- Burkett, Larry. *Debt-Free Living: How to Get Out of Debt and Stay Out*. Chicago: Moody, 2000.

- Burkett, Larry. *The Family Financial Workbook: A Practical Guide to Budgeting*. Chicago: Moody, 2000.

- Crown Financial Ministries
  P.O. Box 2377
  Gainesville, GA 30503-2377
  (800) 722-1976 • (770) 534-1000 www.crown.org

DISCUSSION STARTERS

1. When you were growing up, did your family have any kind of stewardship plan?

2. What have you done to teach the concept of stewardship to your children?

3. Which section of this chapter challenged you the most?

4. What decisions do you need to make as a family about your finances?

5. What is the significance of the following scriptures? How can these words of Jesus help a family with their finances?

For where your treasure is, there your heart will be also. . . . No one can serve two masters. Either he will hate the one and love the other, or he will be devoted to the one and despise the other. You cannot serve both God and Money. (Matt. 6:21, 24)

10

ENERGIZE YOUR FAMILY'S SPIRITUAL GROWTH

I love the lesson this mother learned from her innocent child:

We were the only family with children in the restaurant. I sat Erik in a high chair. Suddenly Erik squealed and said, "Hi there." He pounded his hands on the high chair tray and wriggled and giggled with merriment. I looked around and saw the source of his merriment. It was a man with a tattered rag of a coat, dirty, greasy, and worn. His pants were baggy with a zipper at half-mast, and his toes poked out of would-be shoes. His shirt was dirty and his hair uncombed and unwashed. His whiskers were too short to be called a beard and his nose was so varicose it looked like a road map. We were too far from him to smell, but I was sure he smelled. His hands waved and flapped on loose wrists. "Hi there, baby. I see ya, buster," the man said to Erik. My husband and I exchanged looks, What do we do? Everyone in the restaurant noticed and looked at us and then at the man. The old geezer was creating a nuisance with my beautiful baby. Our meal came and the man began shouting across the room, "Do ya know patty cake? Do ya know peek-a-boo? Hey, look, he knows peek-a-boo." Nobody thought the old man was cute. He was obviously drunk. My husband and I were embarrassed. We ate in silence, all except for Erik, who was running through his repertoire for the admiring skid-row bum, who in turn, reciprocated with his cute comments.

We finally got through the meal and headed for the door. My husband went to pay the check and told me to meet him in the parking lot. The old man sat poised between the door and me. "Lord, just let me out of here before he speaks to me or Erik," I prayed. As I drew closer to the man, I turned my back trying to sidestep him and avoid any air he might be breathing. As I did, Erik leaned over my arm, reaching with both arms in a baby's pick-me-up position. Before I could stop him, Erik had propelled himself from my arms to the man's. Suddenly a very smelly old man and a very young baby consummated their love relationship. Erik, in an act of total trust, love, and submission laid his tiny head upon the man's ragged shoulder. The man's eyes closed and I saw tears hover beneath his lashes. His aged hands full of grime, pain, and hard labor—gently, so gently cradled my baby's bottom and stroked his back. No two beings have ever loved so deeply for so short a time. I stood awestruck. The old man rocked and cradled Erik in his arms for a moment, and then his eyes opened and set squarely on mine. He said in a firm commanding voice, "You take care of this baby." Somehow I managed, "I will," from a throat that contained a stone. He pried Erik from his chest unwillingly, longingly, as though he was in pain. I received my baby and the man said, "God bless you, ma'am, you've just given me my Christmas gift." I said nothing more than a muttered thanks. With Erik in my arm, I ran for the car. My husband was wondering why I was crying and holding Erik so tightly, and why I was saying, "My God, my God, forgive me." I had just witnessed Christ's love shown through the innocence of a tiny child who saw no sin, who made no judgment, a child who saw a soul, and a mother who saw a suit of clothes. I was a Christian who was blind, holding a child who was not. I felt it was God asking, "Are you willing to share your son for a moment?" When He shared His for eternity. The ragged old man, unwittingly, had reminded me that to enter the kingdom of God, we must become as little children.

—Author Unknown

OFTEN WE CAN LEARN SO MUCH about our own spirituality from our children. Their faith is fresh and beautiful. Yet, even though the faith of a child is refreshing, it is so easy for parents to be distracted when it comes to helping our kids grow spiritually.

A woman met with me to talk about her daughter, who was struggling with an eating disorder called anorexia. Basically, the young girl was starving herself to death. During our conversation, the mother mentioned that she had had more than eighteen thousand dollars' worth of cosmetic surgery during the past year. She said she decided to get "everything taken care of at once." She was proud of her new pair of eyes, smaller nose, fuller lips, and larger bra size! When I suggested that her daughter was in dire need of counseling, the mother told me she couldn't afford counseling for her daughter. Wouldn't you agree with me that her priorities were just a bit off?

One of my greatest fears is that families aren't investing the time and energy it takes to leave a spiritual legacy for their children. The average family simply does not take a proactive role in building up the spiritual lives of their children. The same family may spend thousands of dollars and hundreds of hours on important issues like vacations, business plans, and home improvement, but when it comes to spiritual values, we too often allow circumstances and chance to affect how we manage our family life and especially how we handle the spiritual side of our family legacy.

"Unless the LORD builds the house, its builders labor in vain" (Ps. 127:1). That's one of the greatest pieces of advice from the Psalms of the

Old Testament. It is very clear in the Bible that the primary role of a parent is to train children who will not only be faithful to their relationships with God, but also develop their own vital, vibrant faith. Far too many parents expect the church to instill the spiritual values their children need. In a national study done by Family Life Ministries, Christian families expressed that their number one need was assistance in helping their children grow spiritually. Most parents have a difficult time proactively helping their children grow spiritually because they didn't have adequate role models growing up.

YOU SET THE PACE OF SPIRITUAL LEADERSHIP IN YOUR HOME

Usually, a child's faith is very dependent on the examples they see at home. In other words, you set the pace of spiritual leadership in your home. If you desire your children to have vibrant spiritual lives, then they need to see an authentic faith lived out with their family. No one expects you to be perfect, but don't expect them to follow a hypocrite either.

How is your time with God? How long has it been since you gave God a portion of undisturbed, uninterrupted time listening to his voice? We have a photograph of our daughter Heidi sitting on the living room sofa holding the Bible upside down, pretending she was reading it. She could barely walk and definitely couldn't read. When Cathy and I asked her what she was reading, she said, "I'm doing my 'votions." This is the same chair she saw Cathy sitting on with her devotions. Children see; children do.

Apparently, Jesus made time with God an absolute priority. He spent regular time with God, praying and listening. Mark reveals to us, "Very early in the morning, while it was still dark, Jesus got up, left the house and went off to a solitary place, where he prayed" (Mark 1:35). Luke tells us, "Jesus often withdrew to lonely places and prayed" (Luke 5:16). Let me ask the obvious. If Jesus, the Son of God, thought it worthwhile to clear his calendar to pray, wouldn't we be wise to do the same?

I asked one of the busiest women I know how she manages to get so much done in the day. She smiled and showed me her schedule. It read "6:00 A.M.–6:45 A.M. Quiet Time." She had let me in on a secret. Her strength and her stamina came from her time alone with God each morning. One of my hobbies is reading biographies of great women and men of the Christian faith. They come in all shapes, sizes, denominations, and styles, but the one thing they all have in common is a regular, daily time with God.

Do you have a supportive, spiritual accountability relationship? Life is difficult, and living out a vibrant contagious faith is not easy. I find that parents who do a good job of building a spiritual legacy often have a support and accountability system to help them be more effective as the spiritual leaders of the family.

I am currently involved in a weekly support and accountability group with three other men. When we first started the group, we talked about politics and sports and only lightly mentioned our faith and family issues. One day, one of the group members opened up to tell us he was struggling with his marriage, and from that day on, it has been a much more focused, supportive, and deeper sharing group. I will never forget the day I shared that I felt Cathy's and my marriage was a bit "stagnant." When I left the meeting, one of the men called me on my cell phone and said, "You and Cathy need to get away and get some time together. If it's finances or baby-sitting, we'll take care of it. When can you go?" That's the kind of support we all need, even if it is humbling.

Some support and accountability relationships use questions like the ones below to make sure they are keeping on the right track:

- Have you been with a woman/man anywhere this past week that might be seen as compromising?
- Have any of your financial dealings lacked integrity?
- Have you exposed yourself to any sexually explicit material?
- Have you spent adequate time in Bible study and prayer?
- Have you given priority time to your family?
- Have you fulfilled the mandates of your calling?
- Have you just lied to me?

Do you have a person or a group of people with whom you pray on a regular basis? We have found that our involvement with a couples' group from our church has been a wonderful source of friendship, support, and sharing of parenting ideas. Our group is made up of five couples who all have children about the same age. We have studied parenting and marriage resources together, as well as other Bible study materials. It is always amazing how often our parenting, marriage, and spiritual life issues come up no matter what material we are using. In a way, these couples are helping us be better parents to our children and challenging us to build a spiritual legacy.

I remember a season in my life when I was extremely busy and had little accountability. Cathy challenged me by reminding me I had lots of acquaintances and very few friends. She suggested I get together with a man at my work named John. I told her John was way too busy to spend any kind of regular time with me, but she kept pressing me to speak with him. We ended up meeting for lunch every Wednesday for over three years until he moved away. Our Wednesday lunch was never structured.

We talked, shared our week's experiences, discussed perhaps a problem or two, and then prayed together. I loved those times together, and they made me a better husband, father, and focused Christian. Today, John and I see each other every two months because of distance. We keep the relationship close through phone calls and periodic visits. Over the years, those times together have become very meaningful.

If you are married, do you and your spouse have a regular time with God together? Most couples I know struggle with spending quality spiritual times together. It is so easy to get distracted with the pace of life that we miss an essential ingredient to building a spiritual relationship with our spouse. Cathy and I have tried almost every kind of devotional time together, and most of our experiments have fizzled. However, we have come across a method that may not sound "spiritual" enough for some but works for us. First of all, we try to pray daily for our kids and our life. Prayer connects us with God and with each other, and it focuses us on the right priorities of developing the spirituality of our children. Then, we go through a weekly meeting plan that is very conversational and relational. We do not need to prepare ahead of time. We both have our own quiet times and Bible study with God outside of this scheduled meeting with each other. Each week we work through the list below. We would rather have our time together in a peaceful setting, but we have been known to do this weekly meeting while driving, watching one of the children's games, or even on the phone when I am traveling. We both look forward to our weekly spiritual and relational connection. Here's our list:

JIM AND CATHY — WEEKLY MEETING

- Devotional time for the week

- Greatest joy of the week

- Greatest struggles
- An affirmation
- A wish or hope
- Physical goals
- Prayer

Devotional time. This is a chance for us to share with each other what we have been learning. Cathy will often want to contribute something from her Bible study that she thinks relates to me. These moments are often very encouraging and give us a chance to report what spiritual input has come into our life for the week. Because of this time of sharing, we are often looking for something to bring to each other, and it keeps us much more in tune with where we are in our individual journeys with God.

Greatest joy of the week. Usually Cathy shares something that brought her joy centered on the kids. Most of the time my joy is also kid-related. It gives us a chance each week to be reminded of the many blessings we have in our family, ministry, friendships, and events of our life.

Greatest struggle of the week. This can be anything from an irritation to a deep longing, from an in-depth family problem to baring our soul. There have been times when Cathy has said, "My greatest struggle of the week is you." That's when we need to move out of the devotional time and have one of *those conversations* and then come back to devotional time after we have dealt with whatever issue needed to be discussed. I actually look forward to sharing a struggle. It's a great time of support and strength as I share on a deeper level with my spouse.

An affirmation. We try to take a few moments to affirm one another each week. One of my primary love languages (see the discussion on pages 102–4) is affirmation. I know that even with a busy lifestyle, at least once a week Cathy will focus on a quick word of encouragement. It is a great time to reflect on the reasons we married, our partnership with God in parenting our children, and just meeting each other's needs with words of love and encouragement.

A wish or a hope. This can go pretty much in any direction. It can be very deep regarding our relationship with a family member or something as simple as discussing what colors we would like for the new car. I've found this portion of our weekly meeting lighter than the struggle of the week, but often it goes in the same direction.

Physical goals. Both Cathy and I are conscious of the fact that our bodies are the "temple of the Holy Spirit" (1 Cor. 6:19), so we are constantly trying to work on those temples. We take a few moments to share our physical goals with each other and either cheer each other on or help each other to be accountable to our established goals. Through the writing of this book Cathy has had to do more accountability and less cheering as some of the physical disciplines have been lacking in my life.

Prayer. After sharing these different areas of our life with each other and with God, now we are ready to pray. We try to focus on adoration and thanksgiving as well as supplication and requests. Prayer brings couples and families together, and prayer focuses us on our real priorities instead of the false priorities that so often get in the way of seeing the truly important parts of our life.

FOCUS ON THE SPIRITUAL LIFE OF YOUR FAMILY

Why are most families more proactive about sports and school than we are with the spiritual development of our children? Focusing on the spiritual life of our family doesn't come naturally for many families, even those who mean well. Developing children's spiritual lives was a vital part of the Hebrew culture. To this day, the most often quoted scripture in an Orthodox Jewish home is the *Shema,* found in Deuteronomy 6:4–9. They quote parts or all of this passage every morning and evening. It really is the very core of spiritual values for both the Jewish tradition and Christians:

> Hear, O Israel: The LORD our God, the LORD is one. Love the LORD your God with all your heart and with all your soul and with all your strength. These commandments that I give you today are to be upon your hearts. *Impress them on your children.* Talk about them when you sit at home and when you walk along the road, when you lie down and when you get up. Tie them as symbols on your hands and bind them on your foreheads. Write them on the doorframes of your houses and on your gates. (Deut. 6:4–9; emphasis added)

How do we impress the Word of God into the lives of our children? Most parents really haven't done a very good job of passing on their spiritual legacy. Over the years I have asked hundreds of people how or if their families had any kind of spiritual life together, and by far the greatest answer was "We prayed before meals and my parents took us to church and that was about it." I asked the question more out of desperation for my own family than for some type of study.

Neither Cathy nor I grew up in families who were active in church. We didn't have role models in this area of our lives, but we found that even our friends who grew up in pastors' homes didn't have much of a proactive approach to passing the spiritual torch to the next generation either. Some had memories of a rigid devotional time that usually involved their father reading from the Bible or a devotional book. But most just looked blank and didn't have much understanding of how to energize their family's faith.

Today there is a fresh wind of focus on passing our faith to our children in a positive way. Organizations such as Heritage Builders are coming alongside parents to help us light the fire of spiritual growth in our families.[1] Here are two important ideas to foster putting faith into action.

Develop a regular devotional time with your family. As our babies moved toward childhood, Cathy and I tried to start family devotional times. Usually it consisted of my reading the Bible or reading a story. Our kids were usually bored and voiced disapproval. Cathy and I would energetically try for a while, and then we would give up for long periods of time. We kept asking others what devotions they were doing as a family, but everyone in our church and extended relationships simply asked us to give them ideas if we ever came across something that worked. One of the days we pulled the girls together and I read a brief scripture and then a story from one of the devotional books I had written for teenagers. It bombed. In the middle of my story, the girls got in an argument, and Heidi fell asleep. I quit the story in the middle and gave up again!

That night Cathy had an idea. She said, "Jim, with no offense to your devotionals—they are great for teens—the stuff you read isn't age-appropriate or interactive for our girls. I don't blame them for being bored." Ouch!

"What would you do?" I responded.

"Well, I think they have to participate, and we must make them more experiential. Our kids love Sunday school, and that's what they do in their classes."

"Okay, fine. How would you do it?"

"Let's have them act out a Bible story. No one ever said devotions have to be serious, and they definitely don't need a three point sermon." Ouch, again! (It was only two points and a poem anyway.)

So that night we pulled the kids back into Christy's bedroom for what seemed like round one hundred of Burns family devotions. Cathy said, "Tonight we are going to try something different for our family time. I want you to pick out a story and then rehearse it and act it out."

The girls' eyes lit up. Everyone in our family is a frustrated movie star. Christy opened up her Bible storybook, and the first story was about Adam and Eve. "Let's do this one. I want to be Eve." Then the other girls chimed in that they also wanted to be Eve. No one wanted to be Adam; after all, he was a boy. Well, this started an argument between them.

I looked at Cathy and almost smiled that her idea wasn't working either. Then I said to Christy, "You are the oldest. Adam was older than Eve, so you are Adam." She asked if she could draw a mustache on her face, and I said sure. Rebecca and Heidi both still wanted to be Eve. I know some of the Bible scholars reading this book wouldn't like my answer, but I was desperate so I said, "Fine, Rebecca you will be Eve, and Heidi you will be Evette, Eve's little sister." They chose me to be the snake.

The girls went into our bedroom to rehearse, but all I could hear was arguing over what outfits they were going to wear. I still didn't have high hopes for family devotions "Cathy style." Finally, after some prodding, they paraded back into the main stage of Christy's room. Christy came in wearing one of my Hawaiian shirts, a baseball cap, and a mustache painted in permanent marker—but that's another story! Heidi strutted in wearing a Hawaiian hula outfit with the coconut shells for her top so crooked that they weren't covering what they were supposed to cover. The girls had definitely chosen the Hawaiian/Garden of Eden theme. Then six-year-old Rebecca made her appearance as Eve. She was wearing, well, uh, nothing.

Rebecca was absolutely stark naked. She looked at us, put her hands on her hips, and blurted out, "She wasn't wearing anything in the Garden, was she?" I looked at Cathy, and she looked at me. I said, "No, she wasn't, but, Rebecca, if you are ever asked to do this play in Sunday school, you can't wear your birthday suit." Now we were ready to begin the play. As you can imagine, the play was a success, and that's pretty much how our children learned Bible stories. There were no more boring messages from Dad, but every devotional became interactive and experiential.

Now that our children are teenagers we don't do plays, but our family devotionals are still very interactive. Sometimes we let our kids pick what we are going to do because kids support what they help create. We also buy into the philosophy that kids learn best when they talk, not when you talk. What Cathy taught me that day, which has made all the difference in our Burns family times, is to use whatever method your kids will enjoy and is age-appropriate. Lectures and sermons are out; interaction and discussions are in.

If you are having trouble with your family devotional time, then make an appointment with your youth worker or children's director at your church and ask them for their best curriculum ideas or stories that would be age-appropriate for your kids. Make your time fun and spiritual. As you pray together as a family and enjoy each other's company, you will pass on the heritage of faith to your children. The main thing is to have a regular family time together to focus on your faith and follow the biblical mandate in Deuteronomy 6:7 to impress the Word of God on the next generation. (See end of the chapter for five family devotions to get you started with your own family.)

Develop a family constitution. The Constitution of the United States of America documents the foundational laws of governing our country. These are the basic or essential rules to create other laws from in our form of government. If a constitution is important for a country or a value statement is important for a business, then why don't more people create a family constitution? A family constitution is a written list of the important things you and your loved ones want out of your everyday relationships. When you think of your family's values and desires, what words would describe what you would like your family to stand for?

On one of our Burns camping trips, we all took out sheets of paper and began to brainstorm what our "Burns Family Constitution" would look like. Just the activity of sharing ideas was very helpful and, frankly, quite insightful. We then came up with our own family constitution. We have it posted on our refrigerator. Periodically we need to be reminded of the commitment we made to each other to live by our constitution. No matter what the age of your children, let them take an active part in creating your own family constitution. Here is ours:

BURNSES' FAMILY CONSTITUTION

- Honor
- Trust
- Truthfulness and integrity
- Fruit of the Spirit:
    Love, joy, peace, patience,
    kindness, goodness,
    faithfulness, gentleness,
    and self-control

- Support and encouragement
- Time together
- Sharing and generosity
- Respect
- Follow our moral code

Include God's presence in your family renewal. Parents who actively include God's presence in family renewal times are families who will tend to be spiritually healthier than others. These are families who bring the Lord into the daily rituals of life such as bedtimes, mealtimes, driving, and even chores. Children tend to feel more secure in their faith when God is a part of their everyday activities.

Families who include God in their vacations, camps and retreats, books, family nights, and even serving together are families whose children tend to have many happy memories of growing spiritually together. In his excellent book *The Seven Habits of Highly Effective Families*, Stephen Covey emphasizes the importance of family renewal in what he calls "family times" and "one-on-ones." His family renewal involves a look at the total well-being of a family in his diagram below:[2]

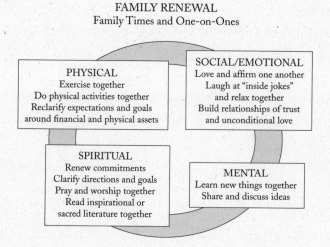

FAMILY RENEWAL
Family Times and One-on-Ones

PHYSICAL
Exercise together
Do physical activities together
Reclarify expectations and goals
around financial and physical assets

SOCIAL/EMOTIONAL
Love and affirm one another
Laugh at "inside jokes"
and relax together
Build relationships of trust
and unconditional love

SPIRITUAL
Renew commitments
Clarify directions and goals
Pray and worship together
Read inspirational or
sacred literature together

MENTAL
Learn new things together
Share and discuss ideas

As you look at this diagram, how is your family doing in each of these areas? What actions can you take to improve your family renewal? Lighting the fires of spiritual growth and wholeness with our children is a daily decision. It takes a great deal of work and energy to pass the torch of our faith to our children. Often there is much we can learn from our kids. Please be assured that it is never too late and definitely never too early to ignite the faith fires in the lives of our family. Our children are not looking for perfection or absolute biblical knowledge, but they do want a spiritual leader who can help show them the way.

As my mother lay in her hospital bed preparing to die of the cancer that had taken over her body, I struggled with the thought of leaving her for one day to speak to six thousand high school students in Colorado. I wanted to be near her when she died. As the time drew near for me to take a plane for this speaking engagement, I was leaning toward not going, since Mom had been so sick. I even asked a friend of mine if he would be willing to fill in for me if I couldn't attend. The conference I was speaking at was kind enough to allow a last-minute replacement if I chose to stay with Mom.

The day before I was scheduled to leave, my mother took a turn for the better. I had not seen her as alert for several weeks. We talked about my trip, and she urged me to "go and help all those kids." She said, "I'll be fine and be right here when you get back." I was torn, but I decided with the prodding of my mom and dad that I should go and speak and return as soon as possible.

I stopped by my parents' home on the way to the airport. Mom was sitting up in her hospital bed. We talked for a short time, and then I turned to leave. She called me back to her bedside and in a weak voice simply said, "Jimmy, I love you, and I'm very, very proud of you." That night after I spoke to the students, I walked back to my hotel room to get a call from Cathy telling me that my mother had died. I made arrangements to fly back to California earlier than planned and tried to sleep. Sometime in the middle of the night I remembered her last words to me. What a blessing. What a spiritual giant. You and I are to carry on the faith to the next generation. It's our highest calling and our God-given mandate.

FURTHER READING

- St. Clair, Barry, and Carol St. Clair. *Ignite the Fire: Kindling a Passion for Christ in Your Kids.* Colorado Springs: Chariot Victor, 1999.

- Trent, John, Rick Osborne, and Kurt Burner. *Parents' Guide to the Spiritual Growth of Children.* Wheaton, Ill.: Tyndale, 2000.

- Tripp, Tedd. *Shepherding a Child's Heart* (Wapwallopen, Pa.: Shepherd Press, 1995).

- Heritage Builders is a ministry designed to help build families of faith. You can find out more about them through their Web site: www.heritagebuilders.org.

DISCUSSION STARTERS

1. Describe the spiritual atmosphere of the home where you grew up.

2. What areas of your own spiritual life could use some help?

3. Have you tried family devotional times? If so, how did it work?

4. As you read the following biblical mandate to pass the faith to our children, what specifically comes to your mind as action steps for your family?

Hear, O Israel: The LORD our God, the LORD is one. Love the LORD your God with all your heart and with all your soul and with all your strength. These commandments that I give you today are to be upon your hearts. Impress them on your children. Talk about them when you sit at home and when you walk along the road, when you lie down and when you get up. Tie them as symbols on your hands and bind them on your foreheads. Write them on the doorframes of your houses and on your gates. (Deut. 6:4–9)

FIVE FAMILY DEVOTIONS

1. Affirmation Bombardment

And let us consider how we may spur one another on toward love and good deeds. Let us not give up meeting together, as some are in the habit of doing, but let us encourage one another—and all the more as you see the Day approaching. (Heb. 10:24–25)

Give words of affirmation and encouragement to each family member one at a time. Some families like to write out three positive encouraging words about each person, share them verbally, and then give the person the papers when finished.

2. Thank Therapy

Give thanks in all circumstances, for this is God's will for you in Christ Jesus. (1 Thess. 5:18)

Have each family member write out ten reasons that he or she is thankful and then share his or her reasons for thankfulness with each other.

---

3. Confession of Sin

If we confess our sins, he is faithful and just and will forgive us our sins and purify us from all unrighteousness. (1 John 1:9)

According to this scripture, as we confess our sins, God forgives us and absolutely cleanses us from those sins. Take a moment to have each family member write out on a piece of paper (privately) his or her sins that come to mind. Have everyone fold up their papers and place them in a safe container. Then burn the papers to signify that God forgives our sins and wipes our slates clean.

Have each family member pray a prayer of thanksgiving for the forgiveness of sin.

4. Rock of Remembrance

Read the following scriptures. What do they say about God? How do they apply to your life?

He is the Rock, his works are perfect, and all his ways are just. A faithful God who does no wrong, upright and just is he. (Deut. 32:4)

The LORD is my rock, my fortress and my deliverer; my God is my rock, in whom I take refuge. He is my shield and the horn of my salvation, my stronghold. (Ps. 18:2)

Many references in the Old Testament show that when the people of Israel had an encounter with God, they would build an altar of rocks to remember God's presence. Have each family member find a rock and then use the rock as a significant commitment to God. Some people use the rock as a way of giving over to the Lord a specific fear or sin. Place the rock in a visible place as a way of remembering this special commitment and time with God.

5. The Encouragement Project

A new command I give you: Love one another. As I have loved you, so you must love one another. (John 13:34)

As a family, choose someone who needs a little encouragement and come up with an idea to bring joy to that person's life. Our family decided to write notes of encouragement to a woman who had lost her husband a year earlier.

NOTES

CHAPTER 1

1. Max Lucado, *When Christ Comes* (Nashville: Word, 1999), 21–22.

CHAPTER 3

1. Monique Nelson, Enough Is Enough Web site, www.enough.org/sharks.htm#Anchor.2 Originally from S. Adams, Sterling Solutions (personal communication, 1 March 1998).
2. For more information, read *Drug-Proof Your Kids* by Stephen Arterburn and Jim Burns (Ventura, Calif.: Regal, 1995).

CHAPTER 4

1. Paul Harvey, *A Wish for a Grandchild*, The Big Picture.
2. James Dobson, Focus on the Family newsletter, February 1994.

CHAPTER 5

1. Richard A. Swenson, *Margin: Restoring Emotional, Physical, Financial, and Time Reserves to Overloaded Lives* (Colorado Springs: NavPress, 1995).
2. Ted W. Engstrom, *The Pursuit of Excellence* (Grand Rapids: Zondervan, 1982), 90.
3. Archibald Hart, *Stress and Your Child* (Nashville: Word, 1992), 8.
4. Ibid., 18–19.

CHAPTER 6

1. Gary Chapman, *The Five Love Languages: How to Express Heartfelt Commitment to Your Mate* (Chicago: Northfield, 1992), 202–203. For more information, read *The Five Love Languages of Children* by Gary Chapman and Ross Campbell, M.D. I highly recommend these books to you.
2. Alex Marlee, "Rate Your Family IQ (Intimacy Quotient)," *Christian Parenting Today*, May/June 1991, 41.

CHAPTER 7
1. Michael Yaconelli, *Dangerous Wonder: The Adventure of Childlike Faith* (Colorado Springs: NavPress, 1998), 72–73.
2. Leonard Sweet, *Learn to Dance the Soul Salsa* (Grand Rapids: Zondervan, 2000), 158.

CHAPTER 8
1. Sweet, *Learn to Dance the Soul Salsa*, 174.
2. Willard F. Harley Jr., *His Needs, Her Needs* (Grand Rapids: Fleming H. Revell, 1988).
3. Chapman, *The Five Love Languages*, 202–3.

CHAPTER 9
1. Ron Blue and Judy Blue, *Money Matters for Parents and Their Kids* (Nashville: Thomas Nelson, 1988).
2. For more information about Compassion International and the child sponsorship program, call (800) 336-7676.

CHAPTER 10
1. Heritage Builders is a ministry designed to help build families of faith. For more information, visit their Web site at www.heritagebuilders.org.
2. Stephen R. Covey, *The Seven Habits of Highly Effective Families* (New York: Golden Books, 1997), 279, 281.